BY A NOSE

BY A NOSE

GAMBLING TALES FROM A HORSERACING INSIDER

JIM GENTILE

The stories contained in this book are my recollections based solely upon my memory. In order to protect the privacy of individuals mentioned in my stories, I have either used only a first name or in some instances a fictitious name was used. In other instances several individuals were combined into one fictitious character for better literary clarity.

Cover: Eye in the Sky Photo provided by William Stoddard, American Teletimer Corp.

Cover Designs and author's photo by Jerri Gentile.

Interior Photo provided by Tom Kinczyk & Jack Lisowski, reprint permission from American Teletimer Corp.

This book was printed in the United States of America.

To order additional copies of this book, contact:
Xlibris Corporation
1-888-795-4274
www.Xlibris.com
Orders@Xlibris.com
54807

DEDICATION

This book is dedicated to my father and mother, Vince and Marion;
to my Aunt Florence and Uncle Dick; and to my Grandma Tess.
All of you made sure you had a good time going through life,
placing a few bets along the way. You've left your
family a legacy of memories and stories
that will span generations.

You can bet we miss you all.

CONTENTS

Preface

I lived in the suburbs of Chicago for most of my life; that is, until I retired to Arizona in November 2005. My formative years were spent in Elmwood Park, an Italian enclave on the west side of the city where my dad and mom raised five rambunctious children in a cozy Georgian. With a gambling history on both sides of the family, we kids were both blessed and cursed. As it turned out, three siblings have a more active "gambling gene" than the other two. No doubt fate intervened when I began working in the horseracing industry in the mid-1970s.

After a thirty-year career at Chicago-area racetracks, my dream job had finally burned me out—and it wasn't just the gambling. When I first started at the track it was like I died and went to heaven. The hours fit my lifestyle, since the only time I got up early was to play golf. Working three to four hours a day at the beginning, and making twice as much as I earned before, seemed like nirvana to me. Besides, I was now getting paid to be where I was spending my free time anyway.

When I started in 1976, there were several positions at the track for which a newcomer could apply. There were the ticket sellers, who sold customers tickets for the upcoming races. Then there were the cashiers, who paid the winning ticket holders after the race was official. These two jobs appealed to most of the clerks because they paid more and were out on the floor in the center of the action. The ticket room and money room jobs were buried in the bowels of the racetrack, where money or tickets were counted all day. In the first thirteen years of my racetrack career, I tried my hand at all of the above. The last seventeen years were spent in the office doing mostly audit work. Since this was a management position, I had scheduled hours and benefits.

Over the years I've shared plenty of track and gambling stories with friends, relatives, and co-workers, who often told me, "You ought to write a book." Since I was better at telling stories than telling jokes, I thought I'd give the book idea a shot. In the past thirty years the subjects of my stories have remained the same, with only my memory to recall the facts. It seemed to me that it was time to immortalize the subjects and the stories in print. This certainly isn't meant to be the great American memoir. Heck, I can't even spell (thank the computer gods for spell-check).

At first I thought I wouldn't have enough material or time to write. Not true; the stories are there, I just have to get them out of my head before it's too late. Plus, now that I'm retired, I definitely have the time. Curiously, writing this book makes me "employed" again, providing I finish it, it gets published, and someone buys it! I don't have enough family to get it on the *New York Times* bestseller list, so I am counting on you, the public, to take a gamble and buy a few copies. Although my friends have heard most of the tales already, I am hoping that they will part with cold hard cash to see themselves and the stories in print!

The tales are as I remember them (and only slightly embellished). Whether you're a gambler or not, I hope you enjoy my tales from the rail and other gambling stories.

Acknowledgments

Writing a book is hard enough, but without collaboration and encouragement it's next to impossible. When I started this book I wrote four chapters and sent them to my cousin, Teresa Brinati. I had known Teresa for more than four decades, and she worked as an editor, so I decided that she would be my litmus test. I could always make her laugh telling my stories, so I figured that if the early chapters held her interest I might be on to something.

Teresa was very supportive and encouraged me to run with it; she told me to send her chapters to read any time, which I did. She thought that my writing style was "breezy" and she made lots of constructive comments about the content. She also checked into some writing groups in Tucson, near where I live in Arizona, in case I wanted to go that route. I decided to continue alone.

After I completed thirty-two separate chapters, Teresa worked her magic, weaving it all into one file and turning it into a readable book. Teresa, you were there in the beginning, and worked overtime in the end, leaving me to my own devices in the middle. Without your insight and input this might have never been possible. Thanks again.

Another cousin who helped gauge the tone of the book was Sister Mary Milano. I kept her in the back of my mind as I worked through the language and stories. If a nun could read this and neither of us had to go to confession, I reached my goal.

After about ten chapters I hit a wall and couldn't write for months. Only my wife, Jerri, and cousin Teresa knew I was writing anything at this point. I was keeping it on the QT. I needed someone else to get me jump started again, so I turned to my longtime friend and one of the original four poker players, Steve Johns.

Growing up, Johns was the funniest guy I knew. Thinking back, I guess it didn't take much to make teenage boys laugh, but even today, when he is on his game, his quick wit is second to none. He used to write the *Card News* (alias *Gnus*) after a night of playing cards with our poker club, which consisted of six guys from the neighborhood (with this particular group, we called each other by our last names). Johns described the game as only he could. The *Gnus* started as a crude two-page synopsis printed on the back of American Family Insurance stationery (Johns was an agent and didn't want to waste the paper). It metamorphosed into a three- to four-page chronicle of our card and golf games, complete with pictures. He incorporated obscure photos of each player as well as other notable figures, inserting bizarre captions that made us laugh out loud. He weaved in each player's stats in cards and golf, which to this day has left an indelible impression.

I think sometimes that our poker club played the game just for the issue of *Card News* that inevitably followed. I recently reread a few back issues of *Gnus* and found that they held their own, like a *Seinfeld* rerun.

Here's another thing about Johns: you could pull a job with him and he would never roll over on you. Translation: Your secret was safe with him. I sent my revised chapters to "Dr. Johns" for a second opinion and the diagnosis came back good. He made writing suggestions, which I incorporated. I continued to send him chapters on a regular basis and awaited his critique. The book was off life support and we were up and running.

With three chapters left, I called Johns and was excited to tell him that I thought I was almost finished writing the book. My excitement was immediately tempered when the good doctor told me that when I was finished I would have to go back and rewrite the whole thing. I said, "What are you talking about? I just spent over a year writing it."

He informed me that when I eventually reread the first chapters, they wouldn't seem as good as when I originally wrote them. Dr. Johns' prognosis was dead-on; the chapters definitely needed work. The later chapters were much better as my writing prowess had progressed. I thank the doctor again for his good advice.

Like one of the nags I bet on, I was stuck in the starting gate and needed someone to help ride this book across the finish line. I knew I couldn't do the rewrites by myself. Who better to turn to than my wife Jerri? She had heard all the stories and experienced some of them first-hand. Being an avid reader, she knows what flows and what would need changing. My wife's contributions and sense of humor got this project completed and eventually published. I thank her for hanging in there while I experienced the events that are chronicled in the book.

There is only one person in these acknowledgements that is still only a voice to me. Paula Paolella used her editing genius to smooth over the rough patches and get my nose to the wire. Thanks for adding your personal touch to the manuscript.

I would also like to thank the cast of characters who have weaved their way in and out of the book, giving me this great material. They say there is no honor among thieves, but a very honorable mention goes to Bilko, Crowley, Frankie, Fred, Lutz, George, Keith, Jerry, Joy, Mark O, Mark Y, Mike, Pat, and Pope, to name just a few.

Special thanks go to Roger, who got me the job at the racetrack where a majority of these stories took place. He also has firsthand knowledge of some of them. No job, no book. Thanks, again Roger.

I thank Tom who gave me a job in the mutuel office, extending my racetrack career. When I started quizzing him about some of my stories, he suspected something was up. He asked me one day: "You're writing a book, aren't you?" I tried to BS him, but "you can't bullshit a bull-shitter," and he saw right through me. Tom's another guy who would do the time alone, so I knew "mum was the word." Thanks, Tom.

I learned how to middle a bet and go the other way to ensure a profit from Tony; he knows all the angles and we shared some good experiences together. Thanks for sharing your knowledge with me.

Jack and I worked together for thirty years at Arlington Park Racetrack, the first fifteen on the windows and the last half in the office. Some of these stories are all too familiar to him. I thank Jack for unknowingly (I think) refreshing my memory on some of them.

Sam and I have been friends since 1954—going on six decades! He played a prominent role in a few chapters. Thanks for the quotes and for being part of this creation.

Last, but not least of all, I would like to thank Bob, my partner in crime betting horses the last five years. Bob, listen up: my bad beats seem trivial next to yours, and for that I thank you.

Okay, in the parlance of horseracing, it's post time.

1

Cards — The Beginning

I was born in 1950, the third child — and first-born son — of Marion and Vincent Gentile. We lived with my maternal grandmother, Tessie, on Neva Avenue in the Montclare neighborhood of Chicago's west side. As a four-year-old boy, our house seemed huge, but years later when I passed by it, my perspective had changed. It looked cramped. Which is probably why, in 1954, with two older siblings (Jacki and Carmelita), a younger brother (Jerry) and my mom pregnant with number five (my sister Mari-Jo), my family left grandma and moved to one of the first suburbs west of Chicago — Elmwood Park. It had long streets lined with brick bungalows and Georgians. My grandmother eventually sold the old house and moved in with my Aunt Isabel (my mom's sister) a few blocks down the street from us.

My card-playing gambling gene came from Grandma Tessie. Her first husband loved to gamble and Tessie always wanted to "shuffle," her word for playing cards. Hearts was the prevailing card game at all major holiday gatherings, with 25 cents being the most at stake per game. With eight players, the winner could net a whopping $1.75, but the bragging rights were worth a lot more. I couldn't get into the game until age twelve, but after that I was a permanent fixture. In the year 2000 — twenty-four years after Tessie passed away — the family boldly upped the ante to $1 and played with thirteen people, four cards each, no blind. The winner cleared $12, what a score! Since these family games involved good-natured screaming and yelling, headaches and sore throats often followed.

Everyone claimed that I was Tessie's favorite. She was a devout Catholic and her nickname for me was "Pope Jim." Our Catholic family had yet to produce a priest and she thought that, although a long shot, I might be it. When we played Hearts together, she never stuck me with the queen of spades, since it counted for thirteen points against the unlucky recipient. My family always cried foul and swore the fix was in, but they learned to live with it. As a gambler herself, maybe Tessie had some insight into my future, so she cut me some breaks early in life. Tessie, I appreciate that; those were good times!

Jump ahead to when I am eighteen years old and working at a toy distributor northwest of the city in suburban Des Plaines, Illinois. The day bosses went home at 5:00 p.m., and those of us on the night shift rushed to finish the day's assignments by 8:00 p.m. so that a poker game could commence. Since I was making $2.25 an hour back then, $20 was a lot to lose in a card game. One day I managed to lose $50, but still owed $20. I didn't have the money, so I visited Tessie in hopes of borrowing the $20 to cover my debt. Instead of her purse, she opened her Catholic Missal, which I assumed she used for Sunday Mass, and tucked between the pages was a crisp double-sawbuck. When she gave it to me, I felt obligated to give her something in return, so I promised her two things. First, that I would pay her back, and second, that I would never play poker again. Tessie was a very smart lady and believed only half of what the "pope" said.

One week later I got in another poker game and won $100—more than I made in an entire week of work at the toy distributor! I was hooked. I paid Tessie back immediately and haven't stopped playing cards since. She didn't need to ask me how I got the money to repay her. She knew. That's probably when she realized that Pope Jim was just a pipedream.

The poker seed was planted when we moved to Elmwood Park in 1954. That's when I met my oldest friend to date, Sam, who lived across the street. Sam and I would spy through the neighbor's basement window and watch Ed and his buddies play cards. This sparked an idea: we'd get our own game going. So at age fifteen we began playing poker. Our games started at Sam's house. His basement was the perfect teenage playground with a pool table, ping-pong table, three slot machines (quarter, dime, and nickel) and the requisite poster of Marilyn Monroe that had a big red bow affixed to it to cover her chest. Lifting up the bow became a tradition.

The card games were played for 5 and 10 cents, so a couple bucks was a big win. One day this kid from down the block won five bucks and quit early. We were pissed and never let him play with us again. But he taught us a valuable lesson: When ahead in poker, take the money and run. This also requires playing with strangers. Another lesson learned is that the longer a player stays at the table, the higher the odds of losing. This especially holds true if the pot is *raked* (the house takes a cut), which we didn't do.

By age sixteen I started playing in a regular poker group that included some of the same guys with whom I continued to play over the next forty years. Games would pop up at any time and one of the players, Johns, was notorious for standing up a date if a card game was in the air. However, that did not seem to affect his social life because he always had dates. The core group consisted of Angelo, Bill, Bob, Mark, Steve, Roger, and me. Benny, Bobby, Dominick, Ed, Jerry, John, and Sam, among others, made regular cameo appearances over the years.

As far as I know, all but two of the card players are still alive today, and that encompasses the dozens that played only once with the group. Only one of the players (that I am aware of) went to jail; this was for embezzling from old ladies to feed his gambling addiction. Not a bad percentage; the rest of us are just semi-degenerates in some form or another.

Later in life, with jobs and responsibilities in tow, we played with a specific time limit per game or a defined number of hands. The designation of "pauper" was also instituted so that no one player could lose too much money. When someone became pauper, besides being humiliated by poor play, he had to wear the hat of the night until redeemed. The embarrassing headgear included a jester's hat, a chicken hat, and a crown of thorns, to name a few. This format helped to keep the games fun, friendly, and avoided hard feelings.

Around 1990 I started keeping stats on the games. We distributed a recap of the game along with Johns' *Card News*. With running totals, over the next fifteen years we knew who the big winners and losers were. I learned two things while keeping those stats. First, whoever wins the most pots will ultimately be one of the big money losers in the long run. Players end up playing way too many pots and the extra wins don't make up for all those times they are second or third. Second lesson: if a player keeps his losing sessions to a minimum, he can make money even winning only half the time.

I continue to play cards in Arizona with the occasional visit to Las Vegas, since my wife's mom lives there now. I've actually remembered and applied those lessons learned, and so far I'm holding my own.

2

Horseracing — The Second Coming

The horse-playing gene came from my father's side of the family. My dad had five older sisters and was particularly close with his sister Florence, a raven-haired dynamo who was never without red lipstick. Her husband, my Uncle Dick, served in the Navy during World War II, where he passed his free time on the ship playing poker and gin rummy. He did well enough to send his entire Navy pay back home to Aunt Florence — quite a sum of money at the time. After the war, Uncle Dick and my dad worked in the book joints. Uncle Dick enjoyed a long career as a bookie — thirty-some years. He got his first real job at age fifty-five, working at the post office. A brother-in-law, Uncle John, was a police commander in Chicago and got him the job. Uncle Dick took the night shift for ten years so he could play the horses at Arlington Park Racetrack during the day with his wife. He worked just long enough to be eligible to collect Social Security at age sixty-five.

My Aunt Florence lived life with great panache, especially betting on horses and playing cards. After serving his country, Uncle Dick thought he was returning home to a comfortable nest egg, only to find out that Aunt Flo did not understand the nest egg concept — she had gambled away every cent. To his credit, as the story was told to me, Uncle Dick went on a four-day bender and Aunt Flo lived to tell the tale.

So, as you can see, the deck was stacked for (against!) me: my dad, Aunt Florence, and Grandma Tessie were all gamblers. I never had a chance, but I didn't know it. Ironically, out of the five kids in my family, my younger brother Jerry and oldest sister Jacki got the recessive genes and don't gamble very much. On the other hand, my sisters Carmelita and Mari-Jo like to place a bet or two, and probably have some bad beat stories of their own to tell. They can write their own books.

The first time I saw Arlington Park Racetrack I was twelve years old. Who knew my future would be decided on that fateful visit? Driving out to the track with my dad felt like it took hours. I remember thinking that the two-lane highway in the middle of the cornfields was a road to no man's land. Arlington is only twenty-five miles northwest from our family home in Elmwood Park, but there were no expressways back in 1962. The traffic was slow, especially as we got closer to the track. The old grandstand building was gigantic and mesmerizing; it could accommodate about forty-five thousand patrons.

Arlington Park was the premier thoroughbred racetrack in metropolitan Chicago. It was the first area track to install the electronic tote system (1933), photo-finish cameras (1936), and electronic starting gates (1940). Arlington was also the first track in Illinois to run races on the turf (grass) in 1934. All the premier trainers and jockeys raced at Arlington's summer meet, which usually ran from Memorial Day until Labor Day. It's hard to explain my excitement on that first day when I entered that racetrack.

The betting age at the time was eighteen, so by law I could only watch. On one race my dad asked me to select two horses and said that he would go to the betting windows and wager a $3 Quinella. He explained that if the horses I picked finished first and second, I would win the Quinella. For my inaugural wager I picked out the two names of the horses that I liked best, and what do you think happened? My horses came in and I had won my first real wager at the tender age of twelve. While my dad was collecting my $88 Quinella (almost 30 to 1 for my money), my young and naïve brain had absolutely no idea where this beginner's luck would lead.

The worst thing that can happen to any new gambler is to win the very first attempt at any game. That first time makes a lasting impression and gives the illusion that winning is easy.

My dad brought me to Arlington Park two or three times a year until I was sixteen. When I could gamble legally at age eighteen, I started going to Maywood Park Racetrack, a harness track ridiculously close to home—only one mile west. Although thoroughbreds were much more exciting to watch, and Arlington Park was by far a more impressive venue, I found it to be much harder to bet on due to the bigger fields—up to twelve horses running in a race.

Harness racing at Maywood Park fielded only eight horses. With the tight turns, the speed horses that could make the lead usually held up. Astute bettors found out that with the half-mile track and a short final stretch, speed on the inside was golden. Unfortunately, this meant the horses were bet down, which generated poor payoffs and made Maywood unpopular with regular gamblers.

Another harness track that I liked to go to was Aurora Downs, about thirty miles southwest of Elmwood Park. This was the first track I ever worked at and the track I was leaving when I was involved in a serious auto accident—a head-on collision on a deserted road on a snowy Saturday night in 1972. There were four of us in an old Chevy that thankfully was built like a tank. Dominick, John, and I were in the front seat and my brother Jerry was in the back with the spare tire (the trunk wouldn't open). The car was totaled and the dashboard was pushed in three feet. It was a miracle no one was seriously injured.

The driver of the car that we collided with had no serious injuries either, but he was driving his friend's car and out with another guy's wife. Needless to say, he wanted to kill me at the hospital. Thank god that my brother-in-law was there to intervene. He was the closest to the scene of the accident and I did not want to call my parents.

Aurora Downs was also where I received my first lesson about the evils of "show" betting (betting on a horse to come in first, second, or third). Most people play to win because it offers the best chance of making any money, as you are paid the best odds. It only takes one or two good-priced winners to come out ahead for the day. Betting on a horse to show is an exercise in futility, as I found out on another memorable night.

My buddies Sam, Steve, and I were at Aurora Downs one Saturday night, and after nine races we were almost broke. We pooled our change and came up with $2.60. Since we needed 60 cents for tolls on the way home, we decided to make one last $2 wager on the tenth race. We picked out the longest shot on the board and invested our last $2. Since this nag was going off at 60 to 1, we played him to show, because we didn't think he could possibly win. That was the flaw in our logic. At that price (60 to 1), if he was close enough to run third (show) maybe he *could* win.

When he crossed the wire in front, he paid $126 to win, $44 to place and $6.60 to show. Yeah, we really cleaned up, making $2.20 each on our bet. We would have walked away with over $40 cash apiece if only we had placed that bet to win instead. If we *would've* made the win bet like we *could've*, we *should've* been ahead for the night.

"Woulda, coulda, shoulda," that was also the title of a book written by Dave Feldman, a renowned handicapper who wrote for the *Chicago Sun-Times* for thirty years. He hit the nail right on the head.

3

This Game Is Easy

During my senior year in high school I began to regularly visit Maywood Park Harness Track. On one of my visits I was placing a wager on a Daily Double (picking horses to win the first two races) when the teller behind the window asked me if I wanted a "winning ticket." I looked at him with surprise and asked, "Who doesn't want the winner?" The teller wanted $4 to punch out two identical $2 tickets, one for me and one for him. I thought about it and figured that worst case I'd lose $4, so I might as well take a chance. I took his ticket along with my original bets and went out to watch the first race. My original horse didn't win so I looked at his ticket and he had the winner of the first race. I was halfway home to winning the Daily Double. The second race went off and the horse I needed for the double won easily. I collected $36 for my $4 investment. Feeling pretty good, I bet a few more races and then left while I was a few bucks up for the night.

The next night I went back to Maywood and searched for my special teller. I approached him with some trepidation because I didn't think that he'd remember me, so I refreshed his memory about the prior night's winning ticket. I proceeded to ask what he liked in tonight's double. After he repeated last night's routine, I ponied up the four bucks.

This time I looked at the ticket and immediately went to another window that sold doubles and bought an extra ticket for myself on his numbers. After that I went out to watch the first race; once again

I had the winner, and ditto for the second race. The double paid $28 and I had it twice! I collected my $56 and, feeling even better, I stayed for a few more races before calling it a night.

The chances of a return trip to Maywood were 100%! By this time I couldn't wait to find my lucky teller. At first I didn't see him and my heart started to beat just a little faster. When I spotted him, I calmed down and went to make the double. This time he remembered me as I approached his window. "Hey kid," he said, "Three's a charm, ready for the holy ghost?" This time he wanted a $4 double for his magic picks, and I certainly wasn't going to question him on it. "No problem," I said, and he punched out two tickets for himself. That didn't bother me because I knew that I was going to go down the line and buy an extra $10 double for myself.

The first race went off and I had no doubt in my mind that my horse was going to cross that finish line out front. I wasn't disappointed and began to calculate how much cash that little ticket would be worth. The second race ran and I was hardly watching my horse cross the finish line because I was already heading to the window to collect my winnings. My head was spinning and I just kept thinking to myself, how long has this game been going on? That double paid only $24, but I had it six times! It was sweet dreams that night.

The next day was Saturday and I went to the matinee races at Maywood. I sought out my golden goose and was prepared to unload on both races and the double. We went through the usual routine, he got his two tickets, and this time, so as not to arouse suspicion, I told him to get me an extra ticket too. Of course, I then proceeded to another window and bought a $20 double and also bet $20 on the first horse to win.

The race went off and the first horse won and paid $6. I collected $60 for the win ticket and bet another $20 to win on the horse in the second race. When he won and paid $8 and the double paid $36, I was living large. My score netted me over $500, and I couldn't wait to get out of there with the money. I was up about $700 in four days! I was sure that I had discovered the Holy Grail and I couldn't wait to tell somebody how easy this game was.

My buddy Sam was home from college and when I left the track I went directly to his house. I rang the doorbell and when he answered I told him I had something to show him that he was never going to believe. Like some clandestine meeting in the movies, I looked right, then left, as if I was being stalked, and then whipped out a wad of cash. His eyes practically bulged out of his head and he immediately asked if I had started selling drugs.

I laughed that off and proceeded to tell him my good luck racetrack story. Sam, being the practical one, decided to be the devil's advocate: Why does this guy give you all these winners when he could just bet them himself? I, of course, couldn't answer that with a logical response. All I knew was that I was $700 in front, and this guy was four for four in the win column. Eight horses in each race meant that there were sixty-four possible double combinations (eight times eight). This teller was giving me only one double combination; therefore I figured that he must've known something. I didn't even want to question why I was the lucky recipient.

After the weekend was over Sam went back to college, and I went back to the track. I couldn't wait until Monday night to continue my winning streak. My conversation with Sam was now only a distant memory and all my concentration was focused on how to capitalize on my good fortune. I remembered hearing that it takes money to make money, so I was loaded for bear.

My only concern, then, was that my lucky teller would take a day off, get sick, or get hit by a bus, God forbid!

My mind was eased as I approached the double windows and there was my teller, Joe, in his usual spot. We were on a first-name basis after that third win. He told me that he would now need a few more tickets. I told Joe to give me $20 worth and $10 for him, figuring that was the cost of doing business. Everything was above board. I paid the $30 and off I went to watch the races.

I also bet $30 to win on the first horse and entertained the idea of my status as a gambler now, a *real* professional. I strolled down the stands toward the wire so I could watch up close and personal, my horse cruising past the finish line. The race went off and my horse broke dead last. I wasn't worried since there was a long way to go. As the field of eight horses turned for home, my horse wasn't even in the picture and ran second to last. He beat only one horse and I couldn't imagine how that happened.

I figured that I'd just bet another $30 on the second race, recoup my first race investment of $60, and then go home. In the second race my horse went off at better than 2 to 1, so I stood to make a small profit when he won.

In this race, things looked much better as my horse was in the lead coming for home. With that short stretch it was in the bag. Unfortunately, the wire couldn't come fast enough and my horse got beat. There went $90 down the drain, but I figured that everybody was entitled to an off day. After all, the second horse *almost* won the race.

Tuesday night proved to be another bad run with a loss of $130. Wednesday was also one for the loss column, but I only lost $90. I was tempted to pass on Thursday, but I reasoned that Joe the teller was due and this could be the start of another winning streak. I had to keep playing; after all, I was still in front.

I decided that this time, if the first horse lost, I'd bet $100 on the second nag. This way I could recoup my losses from the last couple of days all at once. Unfortunately for me, I got my chance. I weaved my way to the $100 booth, where I had never been before. I felt like a big shot, albeit a nervous one, placing that bet. To shorten an already long story, my horse broke stride, lost, and my bankroll shriveled to $250.

My confidence in Joe was approaching zip, zero, and zilch. Friday would be his last shot to get the ship righted. I figured that if the worst case reared its ugly head I'd still be up $180, which is exactly what happened.

As my Holy Grail was slipping away I remembered my buddy Sam's assumptions that Joe was just guessing and the law of averages would catch up to him. Maywood's racing season ended the following week. What a bummer. I figured I'd never get to the truth.

Fast-forward eight years. I am now *working* at Maywood on the main line when I saw a familiar face—Joe's! I refreshed his memory about our history together. We talked awhile and my old mystery was solved. Joe was an ex-trainer of harness horses and also a pretty good handicapper. That's why his doubles never paid a lot because they were just logical choices. Rather than use his own money to place a bet, Joe touted his picks and used other people's money. After all, that's how Donald Trump made his fortune.

Once again, another life lesson learned. Popular expressions—"There is no such thing as a free lunch" and "If it's too good to be true, it probably is"—are more fact than fiction. It's not a bad thing to test those theories, that's where we build some of our life experiences.

4

Lights Out

I remember December 1975 like it was yesterday. My friend Roger had just gotten his union card and was working full time at Maywood Park Racetrack. We had worked together at Playskool since 1968 and often talked about getting jobs together at the track. We heard the pay was good, and since we both spent time there, what could be better?

Roger took that dream by the horns and ran with it. He even had to take up jogging to meet with the right people and get the ball rolling. His relentless drive paid off like a winning Trifecta and he was on his way to our dream career. Before he left Playskool, Roger told me that after he got established he'd get me in the door someday. I was in a dead-end job, but managed to patiently hang on for my turn at the starting gate.

One Saturday, during my waiting period, I was reading the sports page and spotted a horse that I'd been following. Empy was his name and he was running in the tenth race on Maywood Park's day card, which also was the only Trifecta race of the day. Winning the Trifecta required picking the top three finishers in the race. What I really liked about Empy was that he was a pure speed horse at a track that rewarded frontrunners. Had Empy drawn posts 1 through 5 he would have been one of the favorites (low odds). Those inside positions produced more winners. The farther outside posts had the worst winning percentage. That day he unfortunately drew the number 8 post, which had the lowest winning percentage of all, literally the kiss of death at Maywood. My only hope was that if there was no other speed in the race, Empy could jump out to the lead from the 8 hole and go wire to wire (that is, lead from start to finish). The morning line had him listed at 8 to 1 odds of winning, and Empy could possibly go off higher than that.

I bought a program to study the competition. It looked to me like Empy was, in fact, the lone speed for that race. Both dad and Uncle Dick taught me that in any race—thoroughbred or harness—look for a lone speed horse at a price. One of my dad's best plays in thoroughbred racing was a sprinter with speed going a mile for the first time. He loved horses that had a lead of a few lengths coming for home. He always said, "Tired horses can't catch tired horses, so you might as well be the one in front."

Based on the program and the wisdom handed down to me, Empy appeared to be the real thing and a definite play. I was going to bank on Empy—literally. I drew out $125 from my savings account and if Empy was going off at good odds, I'd wheel him on top in the Trifecta. Roger and I had done this a few times before. If your top horse wins at a price, and long shots run second or third, the payoff could be really good.

My brilliant plan was to get a $3 Trifecta wheel ticket at a cost of $126, and then find Roger to see if he wanted to go half with me, which would cut our output to only $63 apiece. Since the Trifecta windows didn't open up until after the sixth race, I ran into Roger at his window before I had a chance to make the bet. In my excitement I told him what I had planned for the last race, and right then and there the wheels came off the wagon. Roger told me he had some inside information: the trainer of a horse called Big Mark told him that his horse was going to win. Naturally, Big Mark just happened to be in the last race and would be running against Empy.

Big Mark had the number 3 post position, but lacked in speed, yet because of a trainer's hot tip I threw my beloved Empy into the trash like a half-eaten doughnut. I now rationalized that Empy couldn't win from that unforgiving number 8 position, and even if he got the lead Big Mark would run him down in the stretch. Right then and there I talked myself out of all my hard work and cast aside the wisdom of the ages. Instead, Roger and I wheeled Big Mark on top in the Trifecta.

Since this isn't a great American mystery novel, I'm sure you've figured out what happened. Empy got out to an easy lead, went wire to wire, and paid $22 to win. The Trifecta paid a whopping $2,300 for a measly $3 investment. Big Mark was bet down to the favorite, probably because the trainer tipped everybody, and he ran off the board. He was a come-from-behind horse that got stuck in the pack.

Apparently I didn't learn from an earlier lesson, the one about things that are too good to be true.

That being said: like a sinner on his knees I confess to still betting on "hot tips" from time to time. At this point, I don't think even three Hail Marys and four Our Fathers are going to absolve me.

Maywood Park Racetrack closed for the season at the end of December, just in time for Hawthorne Racecourse to begin its season. The difference between the two tracks was like night and day. Maywood was speed biased and demanded a good trip. Hawthorne had a quarter-mile stretch that only needed the best horse to win. Speed horses often couldn't handle that long stretch. Hawthorne's track catered more to horses that came from behind.

About the third week in January on a cold Saturday, I spotted Big Mark running at Hawthorne. It's his kind of track and I figured that old boy owed me—$2,300 to be exact! I told my girlfriend, who is now my wife, that we were going out to Hawthorne to make some money. Since Hawthorne had nine—and ten-horse fields, their Trifectas tended to pay better than Maywood's. I set out to right a wrong and took only $126 to get the job done.

We arrived around the third race and needed to wait until after the sixth to make the early bet on the tenth race Trifecta. We stood outside in the cold watching the fourth race finish when the power went out at the track and the grandstands and course became suddenly dark. It was after 9 p.m., and there were still six races to go. The officials at Hawthorne assured the crowd that the outage was temporary and power would be restored in five to ten minutes. Right! An hour-and-a-half later, we were still waiting. How could we leave? I was a man on a mission. By now, it was nearly 10:30 p.m. The bewitching hour of midnight was fast approaching. I tried to figure out if six more races could be run in that time.

Here is where knowing some obscure facts can be dangerous. I knew that in the state of Illinois races could not be run after midnight. A race could be made official after midnight *only* if that gate rolled before the clock struck twelve. That night, with less than ninety minutes to go and the lights still out, I knew it was impossible to get to the race for which I was desperately waiting. So, at 10:45 p.m., I conceded to the freaky power outage, left the track with Jerri, got in the car and drove home.

The next morning, while I was reading the newspaper, I spotted an article about the outage at Hawthorne. The blurb reported that power eventually had been restored around 11:00 p.m. and the track was able to finish *all* the races. The track ran six races in one hour, which means ten minutes apart; and since it took over two minutes to get each race run and official, there were less than eight minutes between posts. I was beginning to develop a knot in my stomach. I should have just put the newspaper down, but of course curiosity got the better of me. My eyes flew to the section in the paper that listed the race results. As I scanned the results for Hawthorne, I saw that Big Mark had won . . . and paid $16.80. The knot in my stomach was now causing my heart to beat faster and blood to race to my head. I was officially in shock. If I had stayed and made my $3 Trifecta wheel, I could have collected $8,800. That's right, not $880, but EIGHT THOUSAND EIGHT HUNDRED DOLLARS. That's what the Trifecta paid.

I usually managed to find a way to lose; now I found a way *not* to win. In one month I had lost out on a chance at $11,100 minus my bets of $252. That would have been more money than I had made the entire previous year. There's an old saying: "Right church, wrong pew." Maybe I'll check out those Hail Marys and Our Fathers after all.

5

Pigeons Are Not Just Birds

In the spring of 1976 I got my first racetrack gig at Aurora Downs in southwest suburban Chicago. Since I didn't have a union card yet, the pay for permit workers was only $30 a day. I could only work on weekends, but that was okay since I still had my day job working in a warehouse. I was a ticket clerk up in the dining room on Saturday nights and when the races went off I could look out the big glass window and watch the harness horses run. I was selling at a $2 across-the-board window (win, place, and show), so all I had to do was punch the number of the horse the customer wanted and collect the $6 wager. The job was a no-brainer, but I was at the track where all the action was.

After working my first summer at Arlington Park as a ticket seller I finally got my union card in the fall. Selling tickets was already losing its excitement, and as "idle hands are the devil's workshop," wagering became part of the workday.

Back then clerks could make a wager now and again as long as they paid for the ticket. When clerks made mistakes punching tickets and the current customers didn't want them, they tried to sell them to other customers before the race went off. Some bought these tickets hoping for a winner. I knew of a clerk who punched a wrong $5 Daily Double and, after numerous attempts to sell it to the public, was stuck with it. That "mistake" came in and the ticket was worth more than $1,800. But that happened only once that I knew of. Such instances were few and far between, more often the stuff of urban legends.

Since I was the new kid on the block I tried to balance every day, which required adding my own money when I made a bet, or made a mistake. The old timers who liked to gamble were short all the time, but as long as they paid up it was no big deal. Sometimes that required a little help from the "juice" man, who was happy to accommodate them when they needed a loan. As long as they paid back the juice (interest on the loan), which was $1 for every $5 loaned, they were okay. They didn't have to pay back the total loan, just the interest. This enabled the collections to keep growing on the original money borrowed. The credit card companies of today are the juice men of yesterday. You don't have to pay the whole amount owed, just the minimum balance. Oh, and don't forget to keep charging so that minimum balance keeps going up. The silver lining as you get deeper into debt is that you can earn various "points," "miles," and "rewards."

On Wednesdays—payday—there were three lines at the in-town tracks: one line to get your check, another line to cash your check, and the third line was to pay back your gambling losses. If you only went to line one, you were way ahead of the game.

When I first started working the in-town tracks, sometimes I was assigned to work in the ticket room. There was a lot of down time since we only counted tickets after each race was finished. The rest of the time we played poker and that was the first time that I cashed my check at the racetrack instead of the bank. After a couple of losing poker sessions, I turned down the chance to work in the ticket room when it was offered to me. The final straw came when five aces showed up in a particular hand, and I had two and someone else had three.

By the end of 1976 I changed jobs, becoming a full-time cashier, a job I truly loved. People collecting on winning wagers were a happier group and the job required a little more brainpower. Instead of using a machine designed to only issue tickets and collect the correct amount of money, I now was determining if a ticket was a winner and what the correct payout should be. This was a manual system and the cashiers were responsible for any errors they made. If they overpaid or paid on a ticket that was doctored (altered to be a winner) the money came out of their pockets.

Every cashier took a bad ticket now and again, and those claiming that they *never* did have very selective memories. Bad tickets were known as "pigeons," and typically taped to the inside of every cashier's moneybox. Like a skull and crossbones, they were there for all to see. I didn't know how they got the name *pigeons*, but putting them in plain sight was a not-too-subtle reminder to pay attention. There were other ways to go short, such as bad math, but taking your first pigeon was similar to a horse breaking its maiden. It was a rite of passage and only then were you considered a seasoned cashier.

When I was first training as a cashier, I didn't have my own personal moneybox. I was using the same box I had used as a seller. All regular cashiers had custom moneyboxes made to their specifications. Some cashiers had more slots for the different denominations of bills. Others liked extra cubbyholes for the tickets. Some were larger than others, but the one thing they all had in common was a lock. Only the cashier had the keys (the box maker gave you two).

I think the cost back then was $25 to $30 per box, but it was well worth it. The first thing a clerk did was put his name on the box. That, and the fact that it was keyed, almost guaranteed that no one would heist it. The affluent cashiers had two moneyboxes made and kept one at each track. It was common for clerks to work what was called a doubleheader, the day thoroughbred card at one track followed by the night harness card at another track. The others (peons) were seen toting their boxes from track to track. I vowed to be a peon for only a short time.

During my first six months of cashing, I was pigeon free. The few times I was short were due to bad math. Then, one day at Sportsman Park, I cashed the wrong race. Here's what happened: the number 5 horse had won the fourth race and I cashed the number 5 from the third race. Every ticket is clearly marked with the date and race number, and a separate tote code is designated for each race. I carelessly forgot to check those markings and instead just looked at the winning horse's number. It was a rookie mistake costing me only $12.80. My first pigeon was embarrassingly displayed on my moneybox.

A couple of weeks later I paid the wrong price on a winning horse. Given a show ticket on the winner, I paid out the place price, which was more money by a couple of dollars. Since I had to turn that ticket in for the show credit, it luckily was not taped up as a reminder.

There is an old superstition that everything comes in threes. At the racetrack, if the same number horse comes in three times, or a jockey wins three races in the same day, it's called the "holy ghost" (a sacrilegious nod to the Trinity in Christianity). It didn't take long for my holy ghost to come when three days later at Maywood Park Racetrack I took my third pigeon. The third time was no charm as it cost me almost two days' pay. At the time I was making $56 a day and the bad ticket was worth $108.

That pigeon was a real eye opener because it was a transposition. An older woman came up to my window to cash the Daily Double. The number 8 horse had won the first race and the number 3 horse won the second. She gave me a Daily Double ticket and I checked the date, code, and numbers, and then paid her $108. I put it in my moneybox and cashed other tickets for patrons.

A couple of customers later I received another double ticket to cash. I went through the same steps and paid off the ticket. When I went to put it in the box on top of the first double ticket, something was not right. This ticket read 8/3 and the one in my moneybox read 3/8. I quickly looked to see which one was correct, and it was the one I had just cashed.

That older woman had given me a bad ticket: either she bet 3/8 and 8/3 for the double and just gave me the wrong one, or she got me. Either way, I was out the money. If she gave me the wrong ticket there was a good chance that she tossed out the real winner. If that was the case, then the state of Illinois ended up with my $108, because they received all uncashed winners at that time. Today the racetracks rightfully get to keep any proceeds from uncashed tickets.

I remember the advice given by an old-time cashier who worked next to me. "Kid, it happens to the best of us," he told me, "Don't let it bother you, it's just the cost of doing business." It would not happen to me again. That pigeon was taped to my box right next to the other one until the day I quit cashing in 1979. I made sure that my display would never turn into a gallery of mistakes.

I finally realized why they called bad tickets pigeons. Like the real birds, there is always more than one and they crap all over everything.

6

Howie and the $100,000 Candy Bar

The year 1979 brought with it a technology change in the horseracing industry. The spring meet opened at Sportsman Park with a new tote system. The Amtote 300 machine allowed clerks to sell and cash at the same window with one machine. No need for separate windows because patrons could now cash and then bet off their winnings at the same time. This was one-stop gambling at its best.

Sportsman Park had put on all available help during that transition period so that both the clerks and the customers could get comfortable with the new system. That honeymoon period lasted only a month. As often happens with new technology, jobs were eliminated and the racetracks eventually cut the number of workers by about 25%.

With summer right around the corner, Arlington Park Racetrack was due to open its meet on Memorial Day weekend. They were the next track to install the new tote system. Since Arlington needed more tellers, operating during the prime time summer meet, they had to train additional clerks. They were fortunate that most of the line clerks were already trained from Sportsman, but their money room staff was starting from scratch. They had to work out all the bugs and try to adjust or redo procedures that would conform to the new system.

The biggest difference between the old and new systems was the balancing of the tellers (line clerks). Under the old system the ticket sellers would turn in their money every race and the money room would compare that to a tote printout to balance. It was quickly known—within a race—if a clerk was short or over according to his or her return. If a clerk happened to be short, money room managers would collect the difference right then and there. If a clerk was over, which did not happen that often, the clerk would get the money back. This kept a tight control on the sellers betting out of the box (punching tickets for themselves) without actually paying for the wager.

Under the old system, cashiers had a lot more leeway because they were not balanced out until the end of the day. Also, there wasn't the lure of a machine right in front of them to make a bet. They had to go out of their way by closing their window and walking down to where the sellers were located. This deterrent stopped some, but not all. If a gambler wants to make a bet, he'll find a way to do it. Besides, they had a box full of "OPM"—other people's money—at their disposal. This resulted in some cashiers being pulled off their windows for too many shortages.

The general rule at all the racetracks was that clerks were responsible for their own shortages and they couldn't work until shortages were paid in full. There were, of course, exceptions to that rule. If a shortage was large enough that the clerk needed to work in order to pay it back, the clerk was put on a payment plan for a specified amount of dollars per week until the debt was erased.

The new tote system lacked the timely audit controls monitoring the cash flow for sellers and cashiers. Under the old tote system the sellers had the means (the machine) to gamble, but were counted every race. The cashiers had the money at their disposal for the day, but no available machine. Now clerks who enjoyed making a personal wager or two had the best of both worlds. Everyone would have his own personal machine to punch the tickets and the entire day to win back any losses. No one would be the wiser as long as they had enough money in their pockets to balance out at day's end.

Upon occasion some clerks wagered and lost more money than they had in their possession. On such occasions it was not uncommon to see these clerks wandering between races looking to borrow cash to "get out of the box" (pay back what they were short). The new system was originally set up to alarm the money room when a particular clerk had too much money in his moneybox (more than $5,000) so they could go get a skim (that is, take excess cash from a window to the money room). This was a customary practice around the sixth race, depending upon the clerk's cash on hand, and it served two purposes:

1. Clerks could expedite their box count at the end of the night.
2. The money room wouldn't have to count everything the next day.

About two months into the meet, under the new-and-improved system, I was working my usual window in the "tunnel." This was a betting area located under the large tote board right in front of the mutuel manager's office. The tunnel was so named because it was long and narrow with a low ceiling. It didn't provide the best of working conditions. Besides Big Brother watching, there was no air conditioning, and it was hell for anyone who was claustrophobic.

The usual suspects were working that day: Jack, Tom, Jacque, Howie, Stormy, George, myself, and others whose names escape me. It was busy and we kept our heads down and punched tickets all day long. The tunnel was the busiest line in the track because of its location. Customers could watch the odds right up until they placed their bets.

During the last couple of races that day some oddities occurred in the payouts. Horses that were favorites in the morning line were winning and paying unusually high prices, while some long shots that could not win were getting bet way down. In the last race of the day, the Trifecta consisted of three logical horses and paid three times what it should have. All of us in the tunnel talked about the unusual prices, but no one had a clue of what had happened.

The next day the rumors were flying. Apparently a clerk was short more than $100,000 betting out of the box. We all wondered how that could happen. It turned out to be simpler than any of us would imagine. The standard procedures in place showed that Howie, one of our fellow tunnel rats, was supposed to return $103,000 at day's end, according to the tote report. His final return was in actuality only about $3,000. Everyone assumed that something had to be wrong with the system so a log of his window was pulled. This showed all the bets that his machine accepted and cashed throughout the day. It was customary to run logs when clerks went short for large sums of money. Management examined the log and tried to figure out what actually happened.

Howie's logged activity appeared to be normal through the first couple of races, with only a few large bets. As the races progressed, however, the bets got larger, running into the thousands of dollars on single horses. It all climaxed in the last race with a $1,000 Trifecta boxing four horses for a total wager of $24,000!

On that fine summer day, when most clerks came to Arlington Park to work, Howie came to play. He started gambling in the first race by betting $100 and, ironically, won the first two races. He must have thought it was his lucky day and increased his wagering. By the last race he was in the box for over $76,000! With only one race left, his only hope was to hit the Trifecta. Hey, what's another $24,000 when you are already stuck 76 large? After losing the last race, Howie turned in his bag of money and went home.

The next day the union steward was asking if anyone had seen Howie. No one had and it was assumed that he took the day off. It took a couple of days before he was found. He was arrested and charged with theft; only it wasn't really theft. His lawyer argued that no money was stolen; he only punched tickets that he couldn't pay for.

The state of Illinois didn't care who paid and who didn't pay; they just wanted their percentage of the handle, about $3,000 (or 3%). The grapevine had it that Howie paid only $1,500 of that amount, and as far as I know Arlington Park never got a dime. If a picture is worth a thousand words, is getting fired for gambling worth $100,000?

You may be wondering what happened to that new built-in warning system that allegedly goes off when a clerk has excessive cash at his window. I can't confirm who made the big faux pas, what really went wrong, when people knew or didn't know, where the blame finally rested, or how they will prevent this from happening again.

I do know that Howie became a folk hero of sorts to us tunnel rats. He disappeared after the incident and rumor was that he went back to his previous career painting houses. The mention of his name often puts a smile on many clerks' faces. He was the only employee I'm aware of that beat the track out of 100k. To add insult to injury, one of my fellow tunnel rats took a Nestlé $100,000 Candy Bar and put it on the mutuel manager's desk. To this day that still gives me a chuckle.

7

Why Bookmakers Drive Cadillacs

One of my favorite movies when I was growing up was *The Sting*. Past posting the bookmakers and double-crossing the bad guys, it had it all—what a great movie. In fact, right after I first started working at Maywood Park Racetrack, Roger and I tried to catch one of the bookies in suburban Elgin asleep at the wheel (literally).

We came up with a scheme to get a bet in after the fact. Roger was at home in Elgin and my part of the sting had me going to Maywood Park. Back in the day before cell phones (I now sound like my father), most racetracks had no public pay phones on site. Maywood Park did not, but there was a pay phone across the street from the track.

Our scam seemed brilliant. I would watch the first race, which went off at 8:00 p.m. sharp. And as soon as the winner crossed the wire, even before it was official, I would sprint out the door to the pay phone. Roger would get the winner from me and call in the bet to his bookie. Two minutes for the race to be run, two minutes for me to get to the phone, and one minute for Roger to call in the bet. This was a one-race scheme only, since the first race was the only one with a specific starting time.

We assumed that if Roger called a few minutes after 8:00 from his home in Elgin (thirty miles from Maywood Park) we might just get a bet in. We didn't want to wager too much for fear of arousing suspicion. We were hoping for a long shot, but that was a rarity at Maywood.

On the way into the track I checked out the pay phone to make sure it was working by calling Roger. To prevent some wayward phone-caller from using the phone during my five-minute time frame, I taped an "Out of Order" note to the front of the phone. All bases were now covered.

Entering the track, I purchased a program and looked at the first race. There was no standout favorite and the tote board confirmed this with the lowest price being 3 to 1. If it stayed this way, by post time we would be in good shape. We had planned to bet according to the odds. At 3 to 1, we would bet $50, and as the odds went up on the winner we could bet less. We weren't trying to be greedy and make a killing, but if it worked we'd try it again.

There were two things that we had no control over: a long photo finish or an inquiry by the stewards. Either one would delay posting the results, in turn delaying the phone call. We were sure that five minutes was the most time we had to make the call. The perfect scenario was a clear-cut winner at about 10 to 1. Bet $20 to win, and no one would be the wiser!

When the race went off I positioned myself at the television camera closest to the main exit. That might take fifteen seconds off my running time. Turning for home the number 5 post horse at 6 to 1 odds had a clear lead. With Maywood's short stretch it looked like it would not be a photo finish.

I kept thinking to myself, "Just don't break stride." As the horse safely crossed the wire I ran for the exit. I was so concerned with getting to the pay phone that I forgot to get my hand stamped which allowed customers re-entry without repaying. Dodging traffic on the busy street, I got to the phone at 8:03 p.m., one minute early. I dialed Roger and gave him the name of the horse and its number. Calling in the bet with the horse's name would be less suspicious.

Roger called in the bet and then called me right back with good news. The bookie had accepted the bet. Since I couldn't get back in the track without paying, I got in my car and drove home. My work was done.

When I got home the phone rang and it was Roger. "I got bad news," he announced. "What happened?" I asked. Apparently, when Roger called, the bookie was asleep and didn't realize what time it was. After hanging up with Roger, the bookie noticed that it was 8:05 p.m., and he called Roger back and told him that there were no bets after post time. Roger's claim of innocence about the time went on deaf ears. There was no bet. The bottom line, I was out the cost of admission, parking, and one program. I still wonder: if Roger had called in a loser, would the bet still have been refused?

Years later, I was telling the story to my Uncle Dick, who had been in the bookmaking business for a long time. He laughed when he heard the tale and said to me, "That's why bookmakers drive Cadillacs and their customers drive Chevys." He then proceeded to tell me the tale of a horse named Linden Tree.

The story of Linden Tree began in January of 1932 at a racetrack in Mexico called Agua Caliente. The track originally opened in December of 1929 in Tijuana, Mexico. It had four partners, including Baron Long, a wealthy Los Angeles nightclub owner. The racetrack was attached to a resort and was popular among Americans, especially Hollywood celebrities, because drinking, gambling, and horseracing were still illegal in most of the neighboring states.

Agua Caliente was one of a few tracks to have the pari-mutuel tote system installed, which became legal in 1927. This system guaranteed an honest payoff as all wagers entered the system and, after the track's takeout and breakage, the rest was distributed to the winners. Pimlico Racetrack in Maryland was the first American track to put in the new system in 1930.

Bookmakers all across the country used the track odds to pay off their customers. They were bound to pay their clients at mutuel odds, which theoretically were a "fair expression of opinion." If a Philadelphia lawyer didn't write that, I don't know who did!

Linden Tree was a well-bred, two-year-old horse that was running at Caliente and was listed in the morning line at 1/3. That meant that if the horse won, for every $3 you bet you would get back $4, winning $1. Such odds made it a very strong favorite, so when Chicago bookmakers received more than $5,000 in action on a promising two-year-old in Mexico, they calculated their losses at less than $2,000 if the horse won. If Linden Tree happened to lose, they stood to make $5,000.

Since Agua Caliente was in Mexico, you could not get a live race call, so everyone had to wait until the results came over the wire. Imagine the look on bookmakers' faces when the results came in with Linden Tree winning at 9.7 to 1 odds and paying $21.40 for every $2 wager ($19.40 + $2 = $21.40). That couldn't be for a horse that was 1/3 in the morning line. All the bookies started calling around town to find out if they had gotten bad results. Since they all received their information from a single source, the General News Bureau, everybody in town had the same payout information.

It was a unanimous decision to hold off on any payoffs until they got a firm confirmation. It appeared that the mutuel odds on Linden Tree were not a "fair expression of opinion." The bookies stood to lose $40,000 on a bet where the downside was supposed to be only around $2,000. They finally received a dispatch from General News Bureau stating: "After a careful investigation, it has been found that trickery was resorted to in the first race at Agua Caliente, we advise our clients to pay off at 1/3."

The investigation revealed that Baron Long, the part owner of Agua Caliente Corporation and a racehorse owner, was responsible. Over the years he apparently got tired of bookmakers sending money to the tracks, cutting down the prices of the horses their clients bet on. He decided to turn the tables on the bookies.

First he bet $1,000 to win on Linden Tree with a bookmaker on the East Coast. Then he bet $3,500 at Agua Caliente, spread out over all the other horses in the race, except Linden Tree. With small mutuel pools this forced the price of Linden Tree up to 9.7/1. He expected to win $9,700 on Linden Tree; with an initial investment of $3,500, his profit would be $6,200.

My Uncle Dick said that most of the bookies in Chicago didn't pay the inflated price. Some might have paid the $2 bettor the $21.40 to keep them happy and coming back, but any wise guys who bet a couple hundred bucks were out of luck. I don't know if Baron Long ever got paid from the East Coast bookies, but causing near heart attacks in the world of bookmaking may have been the only payoff he needed.

Betting a load of money on all the horses in a race except one hardly seems like trickery, sorcery, or whatever else they wanted to call it. The real deception was when the bookies waved a magic wand over their Cadillacs and made big losses disappear right before everyone's eyes.

8

Tommy the Scrubber

While Roger and I unsuccessfully tried to outmaneuver the bookies, Tommy had his sights set on beating the roulette wheel. My buddy Sam owned a grocery store in Cicero, a working class neighborhood on the western edge of Chicago. One day we were talking about Las Vegas and he told me about this kid named Tommy who cleaned the floors in his store one night a week. Apparently he flew to Vegas on a weekly basis for a two-day spree at the roulette wheel and made $20 to $30 an hour. It seemed he had a "roulette theory" and claimed to be making two to three hundred dollars a day when he used his system.

Sam naturally inquired exactly how he was able to beat the casinos at their own game. Before the floor washer would reveal his system, he swore Sam to secrecy. (Because no blood bonding ritual was involved, Sam, of course, immediately told me about it.)

"Tommy the Scrubber" (as we called him) claimed the system was so simple that anyone could master it. Tommy would go to the roulette table and play either even/odd or red/black. There are thirty-eight slots on the American roulette wheel with numbers 1 to 36, half red, half black, and half even, half odd. The other two slots are green in color and numbered 0 and 00. Whatever choice Tommy made (red/black or even/odd), if it lost, that had to be his choice until it won. Any win made all new choices an option. Each bet paid even money, so a $5 bet won $5. If it fell on 0 or double 0, he lost. That, of course, gave the house their edge, but Tommy didn't care about the house advantage because he would double up after every loss. Eventually he would get his money back plus the original bet.

In theory, if Tommy bet black and lost, and red or green (0 and 00) came up, he'd just double down on the next spin and bet $10. If he won he was ahead $5 and would go back to his original bet of $5. If he lost five or six in a row, he'd just keep doubling down until he won. The red/black or the even/odd had to come up at some point. If they spun the wheel thirty times in an hour and Tommy only won four to six sequences in that hour, he would have made $20 to $30 per hour. If he caught a couple red/black, even/odd (whatever he was playing) in a row, he could win more. The key was having enough in his bankroll to survive seven to eight losses in a row.

Some tables had smaller minimums, such as $3 or even $1. One would make less per hour, but could cut down the original bankroll needed. Tommy started with a $5 bet and as the system proved profitable he increased it. An eight-hour workday yielded $160 to $250—tax-free! This certainly beat scrubbing floors for a living.

Now here's where Tommy's system is suspect. All tables have a minimum bet, but they also have a maximum bet. A $5 minimum table would have a $5,000 max bet. That number probably wouldn't mean anything to most people, but to Tommy it should have meant everything. After ten consecutive spins and losses, he would *not* be able to recoup his original bet. Let's do the math. He starts with a $5 bet on the first spin and if he loses, he doubles down on the next spin. By the eleventh spin, he would have to bet $5,120 to win back $5, but the table limit is $5,000, so a win would still cost him $120. Another loss would require a twelfth spin and that bet would have to be $11,240 to win $5; but again, the table limit would prohibit him from even placing the bet.

Tommy the Scrubber either didn't do the math or luck was part of his theory. He obviously never put the "big bettor" scenario into his system since he wasn't one. Maximum wager restrictions are an insurance policy for casinos against the rare, yet sought after, unlimited bankroll.

Even so, after a month of Tommy returning from Vegas a winner, Sam and I tossed around the idea of going with him one weekend and giving his system a try. After all, the town was big enough for the three of us to make money. What bothered Sam and me was that, doing the simple math, we knew that if eleven spins went against us we'd be out of the game *and* money.

Tommy assured Sam that he never had more than seven spins go against him, and therefore never risked more than $635. Since his bankroll was double that amount, he was fine. Now that he was $2,000 ahead, his bankroll had jumped to about $3,300, so he had enough for one extra spin. Tommy was cocksure that he had it all covered and that we were chumps for not getting in on this sure thing. Still, we decided we would wait it out a few more weeks before we pulled the trigger.

The next weekend in Vegas, Tommy the Scrubber's system spun out of control. He was doing well on Saturday, up another $250. On Sunday morning he was up about $50, and then the inevitable happened. The longer a player sits at any table game, the more likely it is that an *anomaly*—something out of the ordinary—will show up. He was playing red on the roulette wheel, when black came up six times in a row. By then Tommy was betting $320 on the seventh spin, which came up green zero. He was down $635 for that run and he needed to bet $640 on the eighth spin to get even plus $5. He then had $1,275 invested and he had never been pushed that far before. When spin number eight came up green double zero, his head almost exploded. In all his weekends of betting, he had never seen two greens in a row show up, and probably didn't want to know what the odds were.

Spin number nine required a bet of $1,280 and would put him down $2,555. He didn't have enough in his bankroll for a tenth spin, which was $2,560, so he really needed a red to come through. The thought crossed his mind to switch to black, but that defeated the purpose of the entire system. While the ball bounced around it landed on red, but only momentarily before it leaped into a black slot like a poisonous frog.

With only $1,045 left in his pocket, he was well short of the $2,560 he needed to wager. Tommy didn't know what to do. The wheel had turned against him ten times in a row! He needed to see one more spin. Making up his mind, he tossed $1,000 on the red, and kept $45 in his pocket for dinner and a cab. The gambling gods proved especially cruel that night as they gave Tommy the heave-ho with another green zero. Out of eleven spins, three were green.

Tommy didn't bother to stick around to see what a twelfth spin would bring. My guess is, with no money at stake, the infamous red would've shown up.

Tommy had fallen prey to a common condition called "Gambler's Fallacy." Simply stated, this is the "incorrect belief that the likelihood of a random event can be affected or predicted from other independent events." All spins of the roulette wheel or tosses of a coin are independent of the last one, unless the coin or wheel is rigged. The "law of averages" is one phrase that gamblers should strike from their vocabulary.

Tommy had started his little experiment with a bankroll of $1,300 and left with $45. Plane fare and hotels could easily have eaten up another $1,000, so the whole shebang cost him roughly $2,300. If Tommy the Scrubber never gambled again, he got away cheap.

9

Got Any Hot Tips?

When I met people outside of work and the conversation turned to my place of employment, inevitably someone would ask, "Got any hot tips?" I suppose this is similar to asking a doctor for a diagnosis during a party or quizzing a lawyer for some free legal advice. I didn't mind. I go by the assumption that the other professions required years of education and training, with full days of testing to determine eligibility. Mine, on the other hand, required a sponsor, an envelope, and a couple hours of instruction. This was "on the job training" all the way.

I don't want to give the impression that racetrack clerks were uneducated. Many were degreed professionals, like myself, but there was a handful who couldn't spell cat if you spotted them the "c" and the "a."

Anyway, for the hot tip question I developed a standard reply: "Yeah, don't bet on the horses." That usually got a laugh, but deep down I got the impression they thought I was holding out on them, keeping all the "winners" for myself.

However, my reply was quite different when I was asked for tips while working my window at the track, "Who do you like in this race?" Looking down at my program I might say, "I like the number 4 horse, bet him straight, put him on top of the 5, 6, 7 in the Trifecta, and box those same numbers in the Exacta" (just like I learned from Joe). If the customer made the bet and it happened to win, I may have created a client relationship. If the bet lost, there was hopefully another "client" only a furlong away.

That's what tellers called the customers that bet with them consistently and asked for opinions or hot tips. Like any relationship, it's a two-way street. When a teller gave out good and profitable information, the client gave a portion of that profit back to the clerk—a tip for a tip. Sometimes a clerk could be overheard telling a co-worker, "I was going to take off tomorrow, but I have a good client coming in and I don't want anyone else getting his hooks into him."

At one time or another all tellers have clients. Some were able to manage several at a time, while others were lucky to get just one. Some tellers recruited clients, like the marines, others just stumbled on them. The whole key to the teller-client relationship was picking winners. Without that, the relationship died.

Some of the bolder tellers didn't wait for a tip, but rather took their "piece" right off the top when the ticket was cashed. Not unlike a fancy restaurant that adds the tip on parties of six or more right to the bill, the tip amount was predetermined.

My own experience with clients was limited since I spent only fifteen years of my thirty-year tenure selling at a window. Also, during those early years, I spent more than half the time working in the money room. Since I never had that military recruiter mentality, the few client relationships that I did have I stumbled upon.

One regular customer, to whom I had given ten straight losers, finally asked me to stop giving him my picks. We came to an agreement that if I no longer offered my "expert" advice he would be happy to throw me a few bucks when he won on his own. He was literally paying me to be quiet. I asked him why he kept betting on my nags. He told me that, applying the law of averages, he figured that I was due for a winner (he hadn't read Chapter 8).

This particular customer liked to bet at my window because I always got his bets correct and he never got shut out. Some clerks were so slow that they would not get bets down in time, and he was a customer who liked to bet late.

Most of my clients were nickel-and-dime bettors ($5 or $10), but I did have one whale. (Racetrack whales are similar to Vegas whales in that they bet more than the average bettor.) One day, while I was working in the tunnel at Arlington Park, a customer approached me to make a wager. I happened to be reading the daily racing form at the time, which is like fishing with very expensive bait. Apparently spending $2 on a racing form bumped me up into the class of serious handicappers.

After feeling a tug on my fishing line, I looked up to see this smiling face at my window asking me if I found any winners in the form. I quickly responded that I liked the number 4 horse in this race. To my amazement he told me to give him $200 to win on number 4. I almost fell off my stool and made him repeat the bet. Two hundred it was, so I punched out the bet.

I looked up at the tote board and noticed that my pick was 5 to 1, making this a nice payoff. I had a rooting interest in the race, but that was not enough as my "hot tip" came in third.

When the whale came back to my window after the race, all I could muster was, "We should have bet him across the board" (win, place, and show). He asked me about the next race, but I told him that I only liked one horse in a later race. I didn't want to burn him out too early. I needed time to study and come up with a winner.

The customer did come back for the later race and this time I suggested $100 to win and $100 to place on the horse I liked. It didn't matter. The horse came in fourth place. As I watched my only whale float away, it appeared I was back to the nickel-and-dime bettors.

So imagine my surprise a couple of days later when my whale shows up before the first race. He wanted to know who I liked in the Daily Double (first two races of the day), so I gave him three horses in the first and two in the second. He bet $20 doubles and had $120 invested. When my picks came in, he collected over $1,100 and our relationship was renewed. He tipped me half a chop ($50) for my expert selections. Thereafter we were formally introduced; his name was George. He gave me a business card for a restaurant he owned on the north side. He usually left before the last race to be there for the dinner crowd. A couple more winners later, and George and I had a good day.

George showed up two or three times a week. We had some good days and some bad days. On the bad days I realized that the dilemma I had with the nickel-and-dime bettors was magnified with the whales. The dilemma was as follows: when a client has a bad day he is usually looking to borrow money to continue betting. After giving him the losers, guess who gets hit up first?

Whenever a customer asks to borrow money at the track, three things can happen, and they are all bad:

1. I tell him I can't lend him any money, and the teller/client relationship is over.
2. I lend him the money and he disappears.
3. I lend the money, get paid back, but my forehead now has ATM stamped on it. This is clearly not a winning situation for the lender.

The first time George asked to borrow money, I offered to give him $100 of the $400 he requested. I didn't want to lose him as a client, but after that I kept no more than $50 on me at any time.

The problem with my whale was that he wanted action in *every* race and I had enough problems trying to pick a couple of winners a day. When I tried to get him to pass a race he would find someone else to give him a horse. The only chance I had to make any money was to give him the winners of the first couple of races. Otherwise he was usually broke by the time he left.

One day Jacque, a teller who worked four windows down from me, stuck his harpoon in my whale and I knew it would be counterproductive. We decided to form a partnership; we pooled whatever we each made from George and did a 50/50 split no matter who gave him the winners. This way each of us had to handicap only half as many races and we could keep the whale in our own bay instead of losing him to the big racetrack ocean.

This arrangement lasted only a short while. Things fell apart the day George was stuck about $2,000 going into the last race. He normally would leave by then, but he was chasing his money. Jacque got him out with a $10 Trifecta and $200 on the winner. After George collected about $2,500, he tried to tip Jacque $40. Jacque went ballistic, refused the $40, wanting a larger cut. George stormed out and from then on avoided us like the plague.

I tried to explain to Jacque that $40 was better than nothing, but he insisted that we were being stiffed. He rationalized that if George collected $2,500, then $40 was an insult. I tried again to make my point with the "bird in the hand is worth two in the bush" analogy. Since Jacque had no idea what that really meant, he didn't share the sentiment.

Whether a client is a small fish or a whale, he seems to believe that clerks have some insight into the outcome of the races. A savvy clerk can pick up subtle changes in betting patterns and use them to his advantage. Others might remember races from weeks ago where horses had bad racing trips and might be ready to win today. The casual bettor cannot know these things.

But the bottom line is that handicapping is a tough game to master. On any given day it's really a crapshoot. As far as "clients" go, sometimes they are more trouble than they're worth.

10

The Fix Is In

My good buddy Sam had this saying from his grandfather: "The only two things on the square are wrestling and horseracing." He'd bring up that old quote whenever we were talking about some sports scandal, like crooked referees or steroids. Obviously, Sam was making the statement tongue in cheek, since he knew wrestling was as choreographed as a performance of *Swan Lake*, and in his mind horseracing ran close to politicians in the honesty department. I wouldn't be too far off base if I said that Sam thought everything was fixed. Another great quote from Sam was "money talks—bullshit walks." Today that's been shortened to "it's all bullshit."

With thousands of races run each racing season at tracks across the United States, including harness, thoroughbred, and quarter horse, it would be safe to say that there are some races that aren't on the square. But to assume that they are *all* fixed is inaccurate. The easiest way to eliminate most "rigged races" is to raise the purse money (the money the top five finishers get paid). This way it becomes more advantageous to try to win the race or finish close to the top.

Disgruntled gamblers think that every race they've lost was fixed, and I'm sure that I've felt that way in the past. I'd be interested in a survey of winners who thought the race they'd just won was not on the up and up. I've personally never heard anyone complain about winning. The reality of it is that a $3,000 claiming race at Beulah Park has a much higher chance of chicanery than any stakes race, allowance race, or a $63,000 maiden race at Saratoga. Nobody pays a lot of money for a horse only to pull him in a race.

Some trainers will bring a new horse along, training him slowly, and they rarely win the first couple of times out. Other trainers will win the first time out of the box. Does that mean that those races were fixed? Absolutely not. The sole benefit to rigging races is financial, and there would have to be at least two parties involved, either individually or together, jockeys and trainers.

A jockey or harness driver can fix a race by losing. They can't win a race with a slow horse, unless the other horses run slower. Sometimes you get what's called a "boat race." This happens when one horse is put on the lead (usually a speed horse) and nobody tries to catch him. In that case, the other jockeys are holding back their horses. Two tip-offs to boat races are: (1) the running time of the race was unusually slow, and (2) the payoff on the winner was unusually large.

Fixes occur more often in harness racing because not all of the drivers need to be involved. Only a few cohorts are necessary to keep the other drivers from winning. Some drivers would ride shotgun next to the eventual winner, keeping everyone else at bay. There were quite a few harness drivers in the Chicagoland area that together worked this scheme to perfection. Maywood Park, because of the track configuration (one-half mile track) was the perfect place for the drivers using these tactics.

Another trick of the harness driver was to "break" his horse on purpose. When a horse breaks stride, the driver is forced to pull out and get back on stride. No advantage can be gained while off stride. Horses that break stride don't often win, especially the ones who aren't trying to in the first place.

If the favorite were to break stride and not hit the board (run first, second, or third), then any payoff on a Trifecta or Exacta would be large. Years ago some of the tellers got to know the harness drivers' runners (those who made the bets for them). Some tellers started following the runners and mimicking their bets, either with their own money or with a client's money.

The drivers noticed that their prices were getting smaller. They started using grandmothers to place their bets (to disguise them) and betting with unsuspecting tellers. It turned into a real game of cat-and-mouse between the drivers and the tellers. With pari-mutuel wagering, the more money bet on any particular combination, the less it will pay. The drivers wanted to keep those winning combinations all to themselves.

Jockeys can lose by putting horses in a bad position on a dead rail (the slow part of the track) or keeping horses wide throughout the race, thus having to run farther. What appears to be a fix is sometimes just a bad ride by a bad jockey. It took me a long time to learn this. The bottom line is: don't bet on bad jockeys. These are easy to spot due to their low winning percentage, usually less than 8%.

Trainers, on the other hand, can get a horse to run faster by "juicing" him with a stimulant or get him to run slower by drugging him. One day at Arlington Park in the 1970s, the Daily Double was cancelled because, in the second race, none of the horses left the starting gate. It appeared that all of the horses were drugged and there was confusion as to which horse was to be the eventual winner. One local trainer lost his license even though the track's explanation for the cancellation was a "faulty starting gate."

When I first started working at Maywood Park's harness track, the old timers would comment after a race that they used "the onion" on the winner. I asked one day what they were talking about and they explained the onion theory. According to racetrack legend, before the race a harness trainer would insert a large onion in the horse's rear end. I asked what that did and was told, "You'd run faster too if I stuck an onion up yours." I had absolutely no argument with that logic. It turns out that the onion functioned as a cheap stimulant. I have often wondered if they used a red onion or the seasonal Vidalia.

In the 1980s there was a huge scandal at the racetracks. The stimulant in vogue then was cocaine, and horses were snorting up like Hollywood celebrities before rehab. This became too costly (ever see the nose on a horse?) and races had more than one horse running "coked up." This era ushered in drug testing, and newer and better drugs were required to stay ahead of the game.

One trainer in Chicago, who had only an average winning percentage, had a knack for putting over two or three price horses the same day. He would then go weeks without a winner. The rumor was that the trainer had someone on the inside of the lab that let him know which day's horses would not be tested, and so he tried to enter his "faster" horses on those days. Nothing was ever proven, but a sharp handicapper could watch for the first winner on the day that the trainer had multiple entrees, and bet the others.

Another racetrack legend that has never been confirmed had to do with the famous "ringer" at Hawthorne Racecourse. A ringer is a horse racing under the name and identity of another, or under a fictitious name. To combat this, horses are tattooed on the inside lip with an identifying number and those numbers are checked before each race. When horses are shipped in from other countries, such as South America, the identities of those horses could be fictitious.

One fall day at Hawthorne there was a South American horse entered in a big race that had poor running lines. The fact that he looked horrible in the form, and was shipped in, enabled him to go off at a large price. After winning the race in impressive time (much faster than his form indicated) there was suspicion that he could be a ringer. Before any action could be taken the horse was shipped out early the next morning.

One might ask why the horse wasn't detained until a further investigation was conducted. Subsequent events offer a possible explanation. On the following morning (November 19, 1978) a fire broke out at the racetrack. Similar to the fire in 1902, it completely destroyed Hawthorne's grandstand, with all horses being evacuated. A cynic might conclude that one incident had something to do with the other.

One way that a trainer and jockey might work in collusion would be to take a horse that has not raced in a while and enter him in a race that he probably can't win. The instructions from the trainer to the jockey might be to run him hard for four or five furlongs and then take him back. This substitutes as a good workout in a live race. The next time out the trainer may drop the horse in class (run against cheaper horses) and try to win at a better mutuel price. I knew a woman handicapper who used to pick a lot of winners using this information. It also helped that she happened to work for some trainers; that's probably where she picked up her handicapping insight.

Working in the tunnel at Arlington, we had a lot of trainers who bet with us. One day I had the good fortune of seeing a really good move. A trainer with whom I was familiar came up to my window and made a four-horse Trifecta box in the last race. After looking at my program to check his numbers, I noticed that he didn't use his own horse in the Trifecta. What was even more alarming was that his horse was the favorite.

When his horse ran off the board and three out of his four-horse box ran 1-2-3, he collected a nice paying Trifecta. In that case, one might correctly assume that "the fix was in."

11

The Chicago White Sox and a Pound of Pot?

During my first seven years at the racetrack, 1976 to 1982, I played horses full time. I kept track of my bets in a book and didn't have a winning year in that entire time frame. I didn't lose much, maybe $1,000 a year, and since I was making a decent salary at the time, it didn't seem like a lot of money to drop. In 1983 I decided to go cold turkey and not make a single bet at the racetrack. My plan was to go to Las Vegas at the end of the year with the $1,000 I would have lost betting at the track. I could blow it all at once in Vegas *and* be on vacation at the same time. By the time March arrived, that "extra" money was burning a hole in my pocket, so I decided to make my first large sports bet.

The Chicago White Sox had a record of 87 wins and 75 losses in 1982. By the time spring training rolled around in 1983, the ball club had added a left-handed pitcher by the name of Floyd Bannister and brought up from the minors a slugging third baseman by the name of Ron Kittle. With eight to ten more wins, the White Sox could capture their division and the next stop would be the pennant. At that time there were two divisions in the American League—East and West. The team with the best record from each division played against each other for the pennant and the right to play the National League pennant winner in the World Series. It may only have been March, but spring training never looked so promising!

The timing was ideal for a large wager. In those days the only way to make a bet was to go to Las Vegas or bet with a bookmaker. At the track someone was always going out to Vegas, but you had to trust him with the bet. A couple of bucks were okay, but I was going to wager $1,000 on the American League pennant and I didn't know anybody that well. I knew guys who bet with the bookmakers all the time and they never had problems getting paid (one caveat: they mostly lost). I got a line on the pennant from Frankie, a guy I worked with at the track. He said that his guy would take a large bet.

The line was 6 to 1, which meant the return would be $6,000 plus the original $1,000 investment if all went well. I gave Frankie the G-note ($1,000) and told him to get me down. At the end of the season, if the White Sox won the pennant, I was looking at $7,000. That's a nice score and all I had to do was lay off horses for the rest of the year, based on my new gambling strategy. Solid logic would have me just quit playing horses and forget the Sox and I'd be $1,000 up at the end of the year, but that thought never crossed my mind.

The first half of the baseball season was uneventful as the Sox were one game over .500 at the All-Star Game break in July. When I saw Frankie at work, he would say things like, "They'll get going in the second half." He was a die-hard Sox fan, so it seemed like true encouragement at the time.

After the All-Star break, the Sox played .500 baseball in their next twenty games, and by the end of July it appeared that I had made another bad bet. The only thing in my favor was that no other team in their division was playing any better, so the Sox were not far out. As August rolled around and the weather got hot, the Sox got hotter. They had 22 wins and only 9 losses in the month of August and were easily in first place. After each victory I would see Frankie at the racetrack and high-five him. I noticed that he didn't seem to be as happy as I was about the Sox winning.

In September the Sox went 13 and 3 to clinch the Western Division on the seventeenth of the month with fourteen games left to play. They didn't stop there and went 11 and 3 to close out the season with a 99-63 record, one win ahead of the Baltimore Orioles, for the best record in both the American and National leagues. This assured them of home field advantage against Baltimore in the five-game playoff series (in 1983, five games were played for the pennant and seven in the World Series). For most of September I did not see much of Frankie; it seemed like he was avoiding me. The few times we did cross paths, I got a "Go Sox!" out of him and then he'd be on his way.

After the Sox clinched the division, I thought Frankie would be ecstatic. After all, he was a diehard. We talked about my wager and he said, "So you get $5,000 if they beat Baltimore." I quickly corrected him and replied that the line was 6 to 1 plus my G-note back for a total of seven grand. He mumbled that I was right and walked away. I had a bad feeling in the pit of my stomach; something wasn't right.

As the regular season wound down, I awaited the playoffs with mixed emotions. As a lifetime Sox fan, I wanted them to beat Baltimore. With a wager on the line, I also wanted to get paid, but I knew that something was not right. I had to find out if my bet was down.

One of my co-workers in the money room at the track was a guy named Mark who knew Frankie really well. I asked Mark to find out about my wager. Mark got right on it. The next day he pulled me in the corner and said, "I got some bad news for you, but remember, don't shoot the messenger." It seems that Frankie didn't place my bet with the bookmaker as promised. Instead he *might have* used my $1,000 to purchase a pound of pot. So my G-note *could have* literally gone up in smoke.

"What about my bet?" I asked, "Am I still down?"

"Well, the good news is that the Sox haven't won yet, so it might be a moot point," Mark replied.

"But what if the Sox beat Baltimore, who's gonna pay me?" I persisted.

Mark looked at me and said, "Life will be simpler if they don't win." So apparently my life would be easier if I was out only $1,000 and not $7,000. Mark had no answer for that.

The White Sox-Orioles series started the next week, and who calls me but Fred, another co-worker. His father was a relief pitcher for the Cubs in the 1940s. Although Fred was a Cubs fan, he had baseball connections and could get four tickets for the first home playoff game. He would use one of the tickets himself, but the other three were mine. I easily rounded up two more Sox fans and we were on for the Friday night game.

The opening game was played in Baltimore on Wednesday, and White Sox ace LaMarr Hoyt pitched a winning five-hitter, going all nine innings. He would be ready for game five on Sunday if necessary. But the next day the Sox were shut out 4 to 0, so that made Friday night's game pivotal. We'd be there to see the Sox first playoff game at home since 1959.

Comiskey Park on Chicago's south side was jammed with ecstatic fans. We barely got to our seats in the upper deck when Baltimore's first baseman, "Steady Eddie" Murray, smacked a three-run homer that sailed over our heads. Richard Dotson, whose 22 and 7 record helped propel the Sox throughout the season, lasted a mere five innings on the mound. The Orioles pummeled the Sox, 11 to 1. Ironically, the Sox had beaten the Dodgers 11 to 0 in the first game of the 1959 World Series. Of course, I was only nine years old at the time, and didn't have $7,000 at stake.

As we headed back to the car after the shellacking, I started to think about the next day's game. Brit Burns was scheduled to pitch and although he had an off year, he had a decent ERA. If we won Saturday's game, we'd have a great shot to win the series on Sunday with LaMarr Hoyt on the mound. His record was 24-10 and he had won the Cy Young Award. I liked our chances in the finale.

Also, there was the problem of collecting on my wager, but I'd cross that bridge when I came to it. If the Sox lost, it's over and done with, and then I am out $1,000.

I wanted to bet something on Baltimore on Saturday's game, but how much? First I'd have to go to another source to get the line on the game, and Mike was the guy. I probably should have used him in the first place. He got me a line with Baltimore at 110. That meant for every $100 I bet I would win $210. Mike didn't require cash up front so I told him to bet $800; if Baltimore won I'd have a profit of $880. The series would be over and I would have lost $120 all total for my aggravation.

But, if the Sox won, I had another problem. I'd be stuck a total of $1,800 going into game five. Now what do I do? If I sit chilly and do nothing on game five I have two outcomes: (1) Sox win and I try to collect $7,000 from Frankie for a profit of $5,200. That option was probably a pipe dream. (2) Sox lose game five and I am out $1,800, but Frankie is off the hook (somebody's happy).

To avoid those outcomes I could bet $2,000 on Baltimore in game five hoping they'd be a slight underdog. If Baltimore won, I'd recoup my $1,800, plus a small profit. If the Sox won, I'm out $2,800 to the bookmakers and $1,000 on my original bet, but I'm owed $7,000 for a profit of $3,200. My only problem would be getting that $7,000 out of Frankie.

At that point I had no idea of which team to root for in Saturday's game. When this all started I was rooting for the Sox, now my head was spinning. What a tangled web this turned out to be.

Because of my job at the track, I could only listen to Saturday's game on the radio. Brit Burns pitched the best game of his career for the Sox, as he shut out the Orioles for the first nine innings. All the Sox needed was one stinking run to win in regulation.

The Sox's best chance came in the eighth inning, with a runner on base. But when shortstop Jerry Dybzinski ran through a stop sign at third base, he was easily thrown out at the plate. When Burns came out to pitch the tenth inning, I knew that it was over. Baltimore scored three runs in the top of the tenth to put us Sox fans out of our misery. It was a great year that ended badly. The Sox would not come this close again for twenty-two years.

Mike collected my $880 for me and I duked him $80 for his trouble. The whole experience cost me $200, but it probably ended for the better. I rationalized that I had $800 in my pocket instead of trying to collect $7,000 from somebody who probably didn't have it. Plus I didn't have to agonize about what to do on Sunday for game five.

Frankie and I never really talked much after the playoffs. To this day I don't know if he knew that I was more than aware of his predicament. Fortunately, no bridges were burned. I did learn one powerful lesson that can be summed up in a single word: RECEIPT. From then on, I vowed that any bets I made would be made with a casino where I would receive a slip of paper with the amount owed me written on it. No more using somebody's "guy"—in Chicago everybody's got a "guy."

You probably thought that the lesson learned was: Stop Gambling. Nope, didn't learn that one. Besides, that's two words.

12

The 1985 Bears and the Super Bowl Shuffle

Growing up in Chicago during the 1950s, there were two kinds of professional football fans: Bears or Cardinals. The Bears played in Wrigley Field, home of the Chicago Cubs baseball team. So if you were a Cubs fan, you were probably a Bears fan, too. The Cardinals played in old Comiskey Park, where the "other" baseball team played. Most White Sox fans were Cardinal fans.

The highlight of the Cardinals' seasons in Comiskey Park came in 1947 when they beat the rival Bears to advance and win the championship. In 1948, after going 11 and 1, they lost to the Eagles 7 to 0 for the title. Some say that George Halas—legendary owner and coach of the Bears—ran the Cardinals out of town after the 1959 season. After eleven losing seasons, the Bidwell's moved their team to St. Louis. The Cardinals were second-class citizens to the Bears, just like the White Sox were second to the Cubs, or so it seemed.

The Cardinals moved the same year—1959—that the White Sox won the pennant and I was just becoming a Sox fan. At age nine, baseball was all I cared about, and since the Bears played in Wrigley I looked for another team to root for. My father was always a Sox and Cardinal fan, but he also liked the Green Bay Packers. We had a distant cousin who played for the Packers in the 1940s—Tony Canadeo—and he was a Hall of Famer.

After the Cardinals left town, we watched Packer games on TV. In the 1960s the Packers dominated with Vince Lombardi as head coach. They won two championships and the first two Super Bowls in 1966 and 1967. One reason that the Bears won in 1968 was because the Packers' spectacular halfback Paul Horning was suspended for gambling. The only two games Green Bay lost were to the Bears, who won the championship.

After winning Super Bowl II in 1967, Lombardi stepped down as coach and the Packers wouldn't be a factor until 1992, when the dawn of the Brett Favre era began. Since the Packers were tough to follow during the '70s and '80s, I started watching the Bears and their new head coach Mike Ditka.

"Da Coach" (he liked to call himself that) was pretty entertaining and the sportswriters loved his sound bites. No one ever knew what he was going to say and he usually blurted out something that was controversial at the time.

In 1984 the Bears looked to be rounding into form, and even though they lost to San Francisco in the playoffs, they appeared to be ready for a good year. Buddy Ryan was the defensive coach and some said he would be the reason the Bears got to the Super Bowl. His players loved him and he was headstrong, just like Ditka.

When William "The Refrigerator" Perry came into camp as the twenty-second pick of the first round in 1985, Buddy Ryan called him a wasted draft choice. He was listed at 6-foot-2-inches and 320 pounds, but looked even bigger, earning him his well-deserved nickname. Ryan's comments irritated Ditka, who then started using Perry on offense as a lead blocker at the goal line for the great running back Walter Payton. During the San Francisco game that season, Ditka called a play giving Perry the ball at the goal line. "The Fridge" rushed for a touchdown and the stadium erupted. It was brilliant coaching, but also payback for the year before when the San Francisco 49ers had used a lineman, Guy McIntyre, to rush for a touchdown against the Bears. Ditka obviously never forgot it.

In a game against Green Bay, Perry rushed for another touchdown, and during the year he even caught a pass for a touchdown. The fans in Chicago loved it, and Ditka gave them what they wanted.

That year was a magical one for the Chicago Bears as they went 15 and 1 with their only loss to the Miami Dolphins on Monday night football. After that loss, several members of the team made the popular video titled "The Super Bowl Shuffle," a true testament to the fact that some white men can't dance.

The Bears became the first team in history to not allow any points in the playoffs when they successively shut out the Giants 21-0 and the Rams 24-0. The Bears would play the New England Patriots in Super Bowl XX in New Orleans. Tickets were being scalped for $500 to $1,000, a ridiculous amount of money in those days. I knew of two season ticket holders who went in opposite directions. Fred used his tickets to go to the Super Bowl and Bob scalped his and watched the game in Chicago. They both thought that they made the right decision.

That year the usual Super Bowl pool was held at the racetrack. The cost was $100 for each square purchased. Roger and I put up $50 apiece and took a single square. The pool paid $2,000 for each of the first three quarters and $4,000 for the final score. The numbers drawn were for the whole game, so we definitely needed good numbers to have a chance to win a quarter.

We drew the number 9 for the NFC team and 0 for the AFC team, meaning that the Bears had to end a quarter with 9, 19, 29, 39, etc., and the Patriots with 0, 10, 20, 30, etc. The best numbers in these pools were combinations of 0, 3, 6 and 7. Those numbers gave you a better chance to win the first quarter and possibly another one. With 9 and 0, we really needed some luck to win anything. The good news was that we had the Bears with the 9 and we knew that they could score; with the Patriots at 0, maybe the Bears could shut them out.

The Patriots took the quickest lead in Super Bowl history as Walter Payton fumbled on the second play of the game and New England ended up with a field goal. So much for the shutout and our '0.' Now we needed another Patriot touchdown to get back to 10.

The Bears countered with a field goal of their own to tie the game. After a New England turnover the Bears kicked another field goal. On the next series of downs the vicious Bear defense forced another turnover.

This is when "Da Coach" had his first brain cramp of the game. Instead of giving the ball to Walter Payton, who carried for 1,551 yards that season and also was the leading rusher in football history at that time with 14,860 yards, Ditka let fullback Matt Suhey run the ball in the end zone for a score. The first quarter ended 13-3. In the pool, who ever had the numbers 3 and 3 won the first $2,000.

In the second quarter the Bears drove to the two-yard line and Jim McMahon, the quarterback, scored on a two-yard run. Again, no Walter Payton. After another Bear field goal, the half ended with the score 23-3 in favor of the Bears. The lucky person with the numbers 3 and 3 in the pool won another $2,000. What did I tell you about those numbers?

Early in the second half the Bears drove down to the one-yard line and again Jim McMahon scored on a one-yard run. Why Perry wasn't blocking for Walter Payton on his way into the end zone, I'll never know. I don't want to take anything away from Jim McMahon; he was the only quarterback to score two rushing touchdowns in a Super Bowl. But Payton earned the right to get a touchdown in a Super Bowl, and the fans were begging for it.

With the score 37-3, and the Bears at the Patriots' one yard line, it was finally time to get Walter Payton his much-deserved touchdown. Clearly, the game was over and the Bears might not have another chance to score. "Da Coach" decided to bring in "The Fridge" to score and forgot about the one player he owed that touchdown to, Walter Payton. Nevertheless, the crowd went wild, and Ditka was center stage once again.

Our 9 and 0 numbers in the pool were pretty much dead. We needed a Bears safety and field goal to get to 49 and a New England touchdown to get to 10.

In the fourth quarter New England scored a meaningless touchdown and got us the 10 we needed. A safety by the Bears plus a field goal would mean a winner for us and we'd reach 49—what a long shot. When the Bears got the safety to bring the score to 46, we were in the hunt.

After another turnover the Bears were inside the ten-yard line with very little time left to play in the game. It was first and goal and "Da Coach" finally woke up to the fact that he passed over Walter Payton on at least three other touchdown opportunities.

Ditka called three straight running plays and all 78,000 fans, and the Patriots themselves, knew Payton was getting the ball. When the third play was a loss back to the ten-yard line, the next logical play was to kick a field goal, which would make the final score 49 to 10. That meant that, in the pool, whoever had the numbers 9 for the Bears and zero for the Patriots would win $4,000. Well, we knew who those lucky bastards were: Jim and Roger.

Instead the Bears handed off to Walter Payton for the fourth straight time, and he was stopped short of the goal line (what a surprise). With little time left, the game ended with a score of Bears 46, Patriots 10.

I remember seeing an interview with Walter after the game. His disappointment in not scoring a touchdown in a Super Bowl was hard to disguise. Being the consummate gentleman, he never outwardly complained or placed blame.

In an interview many years later, Jim McMahon said that he should have changed one of the earlier plays and given the ball to Walter to score. After Payton died in 1999 from liver cancer, Mike Ditka finally admitted that he made a mistake, and regretted not calling a play that would have allowed Walter to get a touchdown earlier in the game.

Unlike Walter Payton, I do complain and place blame. In my mind I believe that if Payton had been given the ball earlier and gotten his score, then that last field goal would have been attempted. If made, Roger and I would have been $4,000 richer.

My lesson learned this time was that a true Green Bay Packers fan couldn't make money on the Bears. Instead, I got Super Bowl shuffled.

A little bit of trivia is in order here: the 1985 Super Bowl was the first one after which the winning coach did not receive the traditional congratulations call from the president of the United States. Maybe Ronald Reagan also had 9 and 0 in the office pool.

13

Dare and Defy

As previously mentioned, it has never been uncommon for clerks to bet the races while working. There were, of course, events that contributed to policies of "no wagering by the clerks while on the job." Case in point: Howie was fired for gambling too much and losing. "Big Louie" was fired for exactly the opposite offense. His crime was betting too much on a winning horse. The scenario seems farfetched, but I'll try to explain the events that made it possible.

With the old tote system prior to 1979, whenever the starting gate opened up, the machines automatically locked. No more bets were allowed into the pools. There were no delays and no way to beat the system. One flaw in the new system was that someone had to physically close the pools. This led to delays, and sometimes pools stayed open well into the race being run. Unless you were paying attention, it would go unnoticed, but the gamblers were always looking for an edge.

This was first picked up at Maywood Park's harness meet. Being a half-mile track, the outside posts were not very profitable unless you knew that the driver of the sulky was going for the lead. As I have mentioned before, horses on the lead won more often than not at Maywood Park because of that half-mile track configuration. The best way for horses in the 6, 7, or 8 post positions to win was by going for the lead.

With a rolling gate opening prior to the start of the race, and the pools being slightly delayed before closing, the sharp gambler had about three seconds to see if any horses jumped to an easy lead. If those horses came from the outside posts it was even better, since they were usually a price (good mutuel odds). A new breed of gamblers, known as "the flashers," was born.

The scam worked like this. One finds a clerk with a window that's close to a TV monitor. Most mutuel lines had televisions behind the lines at either end. The customer would approach the window as the gate was rolling and tell the clerk, "Put in $50 to win and I will tell you the horse number on the off." As the gate opened and the machine was still live, the customer would yell out the number of any horse getting an easy lead, especially if the horse was on the outside.

Now there were a lot of clerks who didn't or couldn't punch very fast, especially on the bell (sounded when the race went off). They were afraid of making a mistake and didn't want to get stuck with the ticket. Others were old enough to be God's father and their fingers just didn't work that fast anymore.

The customer looked for the clerks who could punch fast and whose windows had access to the TVs. If the flasher's horse won, he would take care of the clerk (drop a few dollars). Sometimes horses got to an easy lead and were beat, other times the customer waited too long to call his horse and the machine was locked. There were no written contracts, but the rules were plain and simple: if the customer made money, the teller made money. The windows near the TVs became prime workstations for clerks with nimble fingers.

Once in a blue moon someone fell asleep at the wheel in the tote room and the machines stayed open longer into the race. On rare occasions they were open the entire race. In either case, bets could be made at the self-service machines or a clerk's window as the race was being run.

The clerks that gambled on a daily basis also looked for an opportunity to get a bet in after the bell. "Big Louie" was one of them. His nickname came from the fact that it took two stools to hold him up, one for each cheek. That's the first thing I remember noticing about him when I first saw him at Maywood Park.

Louie was working the intertrack at Maywood one afternoon, and they were simulcasting the thoroughbred races from Sportsman Park in Cicero. If bettors lived close to Maywood, they went there instead of traveling to Cicero. The racing wasn't live, but they could bet and watch the races on the televisions.

In one particular race, Louie was trying to get in a bet in for himself and the race went off. He had clearly punched the ticket after the fact and was amazed when the ticket was issued. He looked up at the TV and saw that his horse, Dare and Defy, had jumped out in front early and was ahead by two lengths. Just for the hell of it he went back and punched another ticket on the lead horse and it also printed up. The machines were open, and as he looked around at the other clerks, no one seemed to be paying attention. Some were watching the race, while others were getting a drink of water or just bullshitting.

Louie's eyes were glued to the television, as the lead horse was ahead by three lengths on the backstretch. He quickly punched in $200 to win, the maximum bet the machine would allow, punched the number of the horse in the lead, and started hitting the repeat button. This feature allowed clerks to issue multiple tickets rapidly, and Louie was working that machine like a construction worker holding a jackhammer.

When the horses turned for home, Louie could hear the golden voice of Phil Georgeff, Chicago's renowned racetrack announcer, and his trademark call, "Here they come spinning out of the turn Dare and Defy draws out by 5." Louie's horse had a five-length lead at one of the shortest racetrack stretch runs in the country. The only way he could lose the race was if the horse fell down.

As the winner approached the wire, Louie was still punching madly and the tickets were flying out of the machine. He stopped when Dare and Defy crossed the finish line in front. His machine total read was more than $10,000, which Louie didn't happen to have in his pocket at the time. He knew that he wouldn't need the money because he could cash the tickets and pocket the difference between what the horse paid and what Louie owed.

Now here's the rub in racing: the more that you bet on a horse, the less he will pay. Betting an extra $200 on a horse to win might not even take a horse down 20 cents from say $10.20 to $10.00. Betting $10,000 extra on Dare and Defy moved his odds from 5 to 1 at the start of the race to 4/5 at the finish. This did not go unnoticed by the betting public as the winner's odds were dropping as his lead was widening down the stretch.

Up in the tote room they also realized that there was a problem with the race and that the pools had remained open. They quickly closed the pools but didn't make the race official. This meant that Louie couldn't cash his tickets and was technically short $10,000.

What Louie didn't know was that the tote room had the ability to track bets and identify the windows from which the bets were made. It also showed the time of the wager, which could be compared to the time that the race went off. Louie's window showed that $10,000 was bet on Dare and Defy *after* the start of the race. Now the only question was who made the bet, a customer or Louie. A count of Louie's moneybox proved that answer: he was more than $10,000 short.

The quick and simple fix was to cancel Louie's winning tickets and take the $10,000 out of the pool. Tote could then re-price the race and the winner would pay $12 to win instead of $3.80. The public would receive the correct payout and the only two remaining problems were Louie and the bad publicity. Firing Louie solved both of those problems and that's exactly what happened.

As a seasoned gambler, Louie should have known that a bet that large would knock down the odds substantially and arouse suspicion. A couple hundred dollars bet on the horse might have slipped through the cracks, and Louie probably had that much money in his pocket to cover the bet. The horse might have dropped from 5 to 1 to 9/2, not enough to arouse suspicion. Worst-case scenario, the tote company freezes all tickets that are bet after the bell and Louie is out a couple hundred dollars. But he still has a job.

Louie disappeared from racing, just like Howie did years earlier. One clerk thought that he saw Louie driving a semi-tractor trailer, but was not positive that it was him until he looked at the inscription written on the truck driver's door. It was three simple words:

"Dare and Defy."

14

Dirty Laundry

Money laundering, the metaphorical "cleaning of money," is the practice of engaging in specific financial transactions in order to conceal the identity, source, and/or destination of money. This is the main operation of any underground economy.

In the past, the term *money laundering* was applied to mean financial transactions involving organized crime and many thought it originated during the Prohibition Era. It was not invented then, but many techniques were refined during that period.

Some thought that the term was derived from gangster Al Capone who used laundry mats to hide his ill-gotten gains. In fact, after Capone was convicted of tax evasion in 1931, mobster Meyer Lansky started transferring funds from Florida's illegal casinos to accounts overseas. He purchased a Swiss bank for just those purposes in 1934.

The racetracks, being a cash business, were ripe for the diversification of money. We had many characters that were believed to be expanding into the laundry industry.

"Joe" the Cigarette Man

A couple of times a week, like clockwork, Joe would show up at the racetrack with a shopping bag full of cartons of cigarettes. He had all brands and the price was right, $3 a carton. In 1979, a carton went for seven bucks, so it was a nice discount. Today a brand-name carton sells for around $35, and includes warnings to smokers about gambling with their lives.

Everybody figured that the cigarettes had to be boosted (stolen) and, sure enough, they were. The ironic part was that Joe was stealing from himself. He owned a mom-and-pop grocery store and he took the cigarettes from his own inventory and sold them at a loss. Why would anyone in his right mind do that? The answer is obvious to those of us in the know: He needed gambling money and was on a short leash from his wife.

The more cigarettes he sold, the more money his business lost. Since Joe was a lousy gambler (and businessman), the grocery store losses mounted each week. Eventually his "smarter half" figured out where the leak in the boat was, and Joe disappeared from the racetrack. It was a sad day for the tellers, since most of them smoked.

The Maywood Park Gypsies

Growing up in Elmwood Park it seemed that everybody was Italian, married to an Italian, or pretending to be Italian. Tales of Gypsies were something that you only read about in history books. They were often described as wandering musicians and fortune tellers.

Maywood Park Harness Track was a familiar haunt for a particular rogue clan: the gambling Gypsies. They would pull up to the track's valet parking in an old Rolls Royce and make their grand entrance. There must have been ten of them piled inside, from little kids to grandparents. This brought back the visual of circus clowns spilling out of a Volkswagen. When the youngest bummed a cigarette from the grandmother, it was the first and last time I saw a grade-schooler smoking in public.

This particular clan claimed to be professional horseplayers and one of the local newspapers even did a story about them. Well, they were professional horseplayers like I was a professional golfer.

They tended to gravitate toward one particular clerk, whom we aptly nicknamed "King of the Gypsies." Although the "King" was a pretty fair harness handicapper and usually kept the Gypsies in action for all ten races, the clan was not making a living betting horses.

What they were doing was funneling monies from other "ventures" into income as professional gamblers. Racetracks never ask where your money comes from; as long as it's green and not counterfeit, it's good. Only when you bet over $10,000 at the same window are you even questioned. Anyone can claim to be a professional horseplayer. All that's needed is a bankroll to get started.

One of the downfalls of dealing with the Gypsies occurred when they tapped out of cash early and the "King" was not in the kingdom. I saw first hand one night what happens when the clan goes broke on a clerk's picks. They then look to "borrow" some money to bet the rest of the races. They started begging, which came in waves, one after another, building into a begging tsunami. They offered rings, watches, and all sorts of questionable jewelry as collateral.

After four races of this non-stop barrage, and with only one race left in the card, I saw something that blew my mind. This old-time clerk—with more than twenty years of experience in the racetrack trenches—gave in. He just couldn't hold off for one more race. The begging was too much and they wore him down. He took $300 out of his pocket and threw it at the head of the clan just so they would stop. He took the jewelry as collateral, knowing full well that it was probably worthless.

Flukey and Willie

I always liked Stevie Ray Vaughn's music. When he and his brother Jimmy Vaughn released the album *Double Trouble*, the song that caught my ear was "Willie the Wimp." The Vaughns recorded the song after thousands of mourners showed up in 1984 for the lavish wake and funeral that Flukey put on for his son Willie "The Wimp."

The wake was a media event in Chicago, as people don't often see the recently departed sitting up and holding the steering wheel of a coffin resembling a Cadillac Seville. It had flashing lights and wheels made of flowers. Willie had rings on his fingers and C-notes rolled up like cigarettes in his hands. He became more famous dead than when he was alive.

Flukey and Willie had a bad reputation on the south side of Chicago. They *allegedly* sold drugs and protection and may have done some pimping on the side. Willie really looked the part sitting up in that Cadillac coffin dressed to the nines. Their thriving business provided plenty of cash, mostly in small bills (fives, tens, and twenties).

The nature of their business caused a problem for them. They had to turn small bills into large bills (hundreds or C-notes) in order to replenish their supplies. Those on the supply side of the business preferred larger denominations. Neither of them could just stroll into any bank with a shopping bag full of cash and ask for hundred dollar bills; that might arouse suspicion. In today's climate of environmental consciousness they would have had the added concern of using paper or plastic.

Flukey and Willie ended up with a different diversification plan than the Gypsies. Willie tried his hand at gambling, but was not a very good horseplayer. He was losing way too much money and not getting enough in return to qualify as a professional horseplayer.

Flukey, being an astute businessman, manipulated the age-old barter system. He retained the services of a racetrack employee who had access to C-notes and was willing to trade for smaller bills. Of course, the "fee" for this transaction was rumored to be anywhere between one and two percent of the total money being exchanged. A willing teller could make up to $200 just for counting and turning in to the money room $10,000 of Flukey's money, as long as he was able to procure enough hundred-dollar bills to complete the barter.

The racetrack is similar to the ocean. A bigger fish will always swallow a little fish, and the biggest fish in turn gobbles him up. A teller on the line could only handle so much of Flukey's money without someone taking notice.

What eventually happened was that the head of the satellite money room, where Flukey was doing business, noticed a certain teller ordering up to $10,000 in large bills and then turning in the same amount in smaller bills.

At the racetrack nothing goes unnoticed; everyone is worried about the next guy and how much he's making on the side. It didn't take long for the money room employee to see what was going on. He cut a better deal with Flukey, as he had access to more C-notes than the teller and the time to count the small bills behind closed doors.

This worked perfectly for Flukey because now he made only one trip to the track a week to turn $30,000 to $40,000 in small money into crisp new $100 bills. What a sweet deal for the money room employee pocketing up to $800 a week in cash.

The "sweet" deal for both parties ended shortly thereafter. On November 18, 1986, Flukey, like his son Willie, was murdered in his car. He was set up by one of his own bodyguards and unfortunately there was no one left to throw him the lavish wake and funeral that he had thrown for his son Willie.

15

Sy—Lord of the Rings

Chicago is a great town for some really *unbelievable* deals. Somebody always has a buddy who knows someone who could get his hands on some "hot" merchandise. The usual explanations for such deals were that "it fell off the back of the truck" or "the price was right."

Racetrack regulars were always wandering in with those too-good-to-be-true deals. One day it would be clothes, another day jewelry, and the next electronics, such as stereos, VCRs, and even TVs. Turning this type of merchandise into betting dollars was a common event.

I tried not to get involved in any of that, because I remembered the "speaker scam" from my teen years in Elmwood Park. Back in the late 1960s, the big scam was selling stereo speakers out of the back of a panel truck. I saw this happen a couple of times and one of my friends got burned.

Picture yourself and your friends minding your own business on your home block when a panel truck pulls up to the curb. Two guys that you've never seen before jump out and open up the back of the truck. Inside there are these huge brand name stereo speakers (in those days, bigger was better), still in the original carton.

The spiel would always be the same: "We were supposed to deliver two, but they put four on the truck by mistake." Then the two guys offer to sell the "extra" speakers at half the original price—a bargain that no one in his or her right mind could pass up.

There are several problems with buying merchandise this way. Two of them are:

1. Without knowing the original price, what exactly is half price?
2. There's no warranty supplied, so if it doesn't work what are you supposed to do?

My friend David fell for this scam and bought the speakers. He paid cash, $100 a speaker, because they didn't take checks. We brought them into his basement and plugged them in to his stereo and all we heard was "the sound of silence." We took the back of one of the speakers off to look for a loose wire and, lo and behold, there were no speakers in the speaker cabinets. In their place were cardboard cones behind the black mesh covering, making them look like real speakers from the outside. As you can imagine, David was pissed off, but there was nothing he could do, the perps were long gone.

About a year later I was with another friend of mine, Bobby, and we were sitting on his front steps when a panel truck stopped in front of the house. Out jumped two different scam artists and they went through the same spiel that I heard before with David.

Bobby seemed interested, so I asked these jokers for the original price tag and the warranty card inside the box. With that simple request, they left as quickly as they had arrived, probably re-baiting their hook for a new fish. After they left I filled Bobby in on the scam and he was relieved.

It was the stereo speaker memory that kept me away from 99% of the so-called hot deals that were offered at the racetrack. Not all the merchandise was bad, but some of it was just stolen and sold at a "five-finger" discount price. I felt better avoiding the whole scene and had done a pretty good job of it.

Then I saw the ring. My wife and I were shopping at the mall, which is something I try to keep to a rare occasion. I told her I was looking for a ring and I wanted something different than the usual racetrack fare. Most of the guys had the standard diamond horseshoe ring that was worn on the right pinky finger. I was looking for something unique that could be worn on the fourth digit, since I'm really not a fifth-digit kind of guy.

We went into J.B. Robinson, one of the local jewelers in Chicago, and were looking at men's rings in one of the catalogs. When my wife shopped for jewelry she looked for the three C's: color, cut, and clarity. I, on the other hand, looked for cheap, cheaper, and cheapest.

In the catalog I spotted a ring that was so unusual, I had never seen anything like it before. It resembled a miniature roulette wheel with a small diamond that floated around the wheel as you moved your hand. It was a special order ring that cost more than $1,000.

I was sure no one would have a ring like that and it would be a real conversation piece. But I didn't want to spend that kind of money even though I really liked the ring. So I didn't buy it, but kept thinking about it.

A couple of weeks later I was describing the ring to one of my co-workers in the money room. I told him that it was a great ring but I couldn't justify spending that kind of dough. He told me to go see "Sy, Lord of the Rings." He could get any ring, made to order; he just needed to see a picture. The best part was that it would be half the price that the local jeweler would charge. Sounded like a good deal to me!

With the picture of the ring in hand, I was off on my quest to find Sy, who was a part-time clerk/jeweler. He was a *retired* bailiff from a Chicago suburb. It was rumored that the unwritten job description included occasional discreet procurement and delivery of cash in return for favorable decisions. Or, simply stated, the bailiff was the alleged bagman who funneled the money up to the judge.

In the 1980s, when the feds cracked down on certain judges for fixing cases, especially in traffic court, someone had to take the fall. Sy was one of those "fall guys" who was rewarded with an all-expenses-paid vacation provided by the government. Unfortunately for Sy, it lasted much longer than a week and the accommodations weren't exactly Club Med.

In Chicago, when someone quietly did their time, they usually had a job waiting for them when released. Some ideal job placements were in McCormick Place Convention Center, the Merchandise Mart, and the racetrack. The racetrack fit nicely into Sy's new life, and jewelry was one of his many sidelines.

I approached Sy and told him who sent me. It's always best to be recommended in these types of transactions. After looking at the picture of the ring, the first thing he said was "that ring must go for two grand." A little over $1,000, I replied without missing a beat.

He started at $700. I only wanted to spend $500. We eventually settled on $600, with $300 down so I wouldn't walk away from the deal. The ring would be done in two weeks, and he assured me I wouldn't be disappointed.

Two weeks to the day, Sy came into the money room with the masterpiece in hand. He opened the small ring box and there it was—a miniature roulette wheel with a floating diamond that spun around. "Looks exactly like the one in the catalog and about half the price," he exclaimed.

They say that a picture is worth a thousand words. In this case, the picture never communicated the actual size of the ring. The catalog only showed it from the top; there was no side view, making it impossible to tell how high the ring actually was. "The Lord of the Rings" masterpiece seemed to be almost an inch tall. When I questioned Sy on the ridiculous height of the ring, he informed me that it had to be that way for the mechanism to make the diamond rotate.

Having never seen the original ring, I had nothing to compare it with. I was screwed. After years of avoiding all the other scams and merchandise, I was finally sucked in. Now it was a matter of being out $300 with nothing to show for it or coming up with $300 more and having the "ring." I paid the piper and took the thing home.

My wife took one look at it and with a look of horror on her face demanded to know, "What the hell is that?" We discussed various options and decided that wearing a ring that looked like a top hat on my finger probably wasn't the way to go. She never said, "I told you so" out loud, but any married guy knows the "I told you so" vibe. She didn't have to say anything. I already knew that I somehow managed to scam myself.

Over the next week or so I actually tried to wear the ring, thinking that maybe I would get used to it. When I noticed people trying their best not to laugh, it was time to put the ring away. A month or so later the bad memory started to fade.

Out of the blue my friend in the money room asked me about the ring. As I was too embarrassed to show him the ring originally, I told him the story and proclaimed, "It looks like I learned a $600 lesson the hard way." He felt bad about it and told me to go see

Chuckie, an old timer who worked at the track. He supposedly could off (sell) the ring and get most of my money back.

Chuckie and I actually went way back. We used to gamble together when I first started out at the track. On days when we didn't get picked up (called to work) we'd bet horses. He was the first guy I knew who picked up on horses using Lasik. He knew that Lasik controlled the lung bleeding that occurs in racehorses and they performed better the first time that it was administered. He knew all the angles; so I was hoping that selling the ring wouldn't be a problem.

I found Chuckie and renewed our old acquaintance, talking about our days on the bricks together (waiting to work). When I showed him the ring he asked, "How much do you have into this monstrosity?" When I told him it was $600, he gave me the look. "I thought I taught you better than that," he said. I just shrugged my shoulders and said, "Help me out here, Chuck."

After gazing at the ring for a few seconds he responded, "I got a guy in mind who I might be able to unload this on, but $600's out. I'll see if I can get you $400 for 'old time's sake,' but anything over that is mine."

I told him I would appreciate anything he could do and handed over the ring. It was worth a $200 loss to put this baby to bed.

A couple of days later Chuckie came up to me and peeled off four Benjamins (hundred dollar bills) and greased my palm. "That was quick. Did you do okay on your end?" I asked. He gave me a smile that led me to believe that I should have held out for more.

I didn't ask Chuckie who bought the ring, but that question was answered about six months later. I was selling at a window at Arlington Park Racetrack on a Saturday afternoon when a customer came up to make a bet. He was about six foot four, 300 pounds, and had hands as big as baseball gloves. Sitting on his right pinky finger was my roulette ring.

After making his bet I said, "Nice ring." He smiled and said, "Thanks." After he left the window I thought to myself that the ring actually looked good on him. Some guys are better built for the big bling.

16

Gamblers' Fuzzy Logic

A fellow racetrack clerk presented me with a classic example of what I called "gamblers' fuzzy logic." Sammy frequently flew out to Las Vegas specifically to play blackjack. One day we got talking about his special money management system, which he claimed showed a profit. Since the house's advantage can be up to 5% in blackjack, it is one of many games with an expected negative return, depending on one's playing ability. Needless to say, I was quite interested in his blackjack theory.

Sammy explained his betting system to me and it basically had to do with doubling up at certain times and cutting the bet in half at others. The key element of the plan was to leave the table after three losses in a row. After hearing this, the sure-fire roulette system used by Tommy the Scrubber flashed across my mind. It seemed to me that if Sammy couldn't put the deck in his favor by counting cards, this system would be doomed to failure.

The more one plays, the more one will "regress to the mean." If that mean is an expected loss based on the house percentage, then one must eventually lose. If neither of us counts cards and both play correctly using optimal play (which allows the gambler to decrease the house odds), then the only thing that Sammy's money management system can do for him is to help him lose his money at a slower pace than me. But we both have to lose in the long run because that pesky negative return will eventually rear its ugly head.

I had another friend named Frank who solved his own blackjack dilemma. He would go to the table and whatever his bankroll was, say $200 for that sitting, he would wager that on the first bet. If he won, he doubled his money (or if blackjack came up, increased it by 150%). If he lost, he reasoned that sitting there for a couple of hours would have ground up the $200 anyway. This was apparently much less aggravating for him.

In my opinion, Las Vegas games are grouped into three categories: games of chance, games of semi-skill, and games of mostly skill. The games of chance are Keno, slots, bingo, roulette, and big wheel. The odds are stacked against the player and there is minimal thought involved.

Slot machines have typically been one of the largest revenue building games for the casinos. The old one-arm bandits have been fully automated. Slot junkies only have to press the button marked "max bet" and things automatically spin. No more coins going in or out; the machine takes cash and pays vouchers. God forbid we slow down the gambler: the faster one plays the more one can lose, once again regressing to the mean and that mean is still an expected loss. That being said, I know people who hit more than their fair share of jackpots, while others, like my wife and myself, have never hit one! My wife swears that she is genetically challenged when it comes to any type of gambling.

Some games of semi-skill are craps, blackjack, video poker, let it ride, and three-card poker. You can increase your odds by using optimal play, but still can't erase the house advantage (some would list craps as a game of chance). I had tried optimal play in blackjack for years and never won a dime. In fact, I wish I had $100 for every time I doubled down on 10 or 11 with the dealer showing a 5 or 6 and I still got beat. Even though this strategy mathematically favors the player, I believe I won less than 50% of the time. In semi-skill games the players will last longer, but still are destined to lose in the long run. But as someone once said, "In the long run we are all dead," and I can't dispute that; I just don't want my money to leave before me.

The games that involve more skill than luck are sports betting, card counting in blackjack, poker, and horseracing. These still may be considered games of chance depending on the gambler's skill level. Casinos would like to tell you that card counting is cheating, but if you've ever tried to memorize cards, then you know it isn't easy. It takes skill and concentration, plus counters only receive a small advantage over the house (although a fortune could be made with big enough bets).

In poker and horseracing, people are betting against each other with the house taking a set amount. Poker is easily taught, but a hard game to master. If you are smarter than the Average Joe you could make a living at it, but it takes a lot of work. In horseracing the average take out is 20%. For every dollar that you wager the average return is 80 cents; that's a huge obstacle to overcome. That's why only 3% to 5% of all horseplayers make any money. Horseplayers have their own unique fuzzy logic. The regular horseplayer would rather wager and lose than pass a winning bet. If you don't grasp that notion then you probably fall into one of the other two categories: you don't bet horses very much, and when you do, it's probably just for fun; or you're a really serious player and handicapper and try to ignore the chatter from the wannabes.

Here's an example of my theory. Someone gets a tip on a hot horse. The tip could come from a jockey, agent, trainer, fellow gambler, or someone's brother-in-law. It doesn't matter who it came from. What does matter is that everybody is talking about the hot tip.

The horse is running in the fourth race and his name is "Bob's Bad Luck." As the race approaches there are two options: bet or pass. It seems simple, but it's not. Experience may tell you that these hot horses seldom win, and when they do they don't pay very much. A professional gambler would pass the race and if the horse wins, so what. An ordinary horseplayer, even knowing the outcome, would rather bet the loser than pass the winner.

Crazy, you say? Here's the fuzzy logic: If you pass and the horse wins, then everybody is running around cheering and asking, "How much did you have on him?" At that point you have to lie and say, "Just a double sawbuck." You could never, ever admit that you didn't bet on "Bob's Bad Luck." What you would hear then is: "What's wrong with you? I told you it was good information and he'd win." But if you bet on that horse and he loses, then everybody is in the same boat. Misery loves company.

This same logic can be applied to lottery jackpots. In some workplaces, when the lottery reaches a certain value, everybody throws in $5 or $10 and the group purchases a couple hundred dollars worth of tickets. The reality is that it only *slightly* increases the terrible lotto odds, even though it seems like you have a better chance. Some of these particular workplace groups have won lotto's in the past.

When Wisconsin's Powerball lottery would reach $100 million, someone at the racetrack would drive across the state border and buy tickets for our group. The first time they asked me if I wanted in, I threw in the required $5. The next time they went I was off work and couldn't contribute. After I came in the following day, Bilko, one of the tote guys, told me that he threw in $5 for me, asking me if that was okay. I told him that whenever they collect for the lotto, ALWAYS PUT ME IN. Even though the chances of us winning are slim to none (and slim left town), don't ever leave me out of the action.

How would you like to be the guy who didn't throw $5 in the pool when everyone else walked out the door with a couple of million bucks? I believe my exact words were closer to: "You're not leaving me behind, #*%&*." That $5 was a small price to pay for insurance and the peace of mind that I wouldn't be the only one not celebrating. Bet and lose, or pass up a win, I will choose to bet before passing any day.

Speaking of the lotto we had a few big winners show up at the racetrack over the years. The one that I really remember was this old, broken-down horseplayer who used to bet with the clerks at Trackside. He was always tapping out and borrowing money, which he paid back the next time he came out. After one particular losing night, he left with $10 in his pocket. On the way home he spent $5 for gas, $2 for tolls, and $3 for lotto tickets. The next day he was $9 million richer.

The money didn't seem to change him as a person, as far as I could tell. He still came out to bet horses, although he bet more and was dressed a little nicer. He always remembered the clerks and tipped generously or actually bought us tickets on some of his picks.

On occasion one of his picks would actually win, but that's not the reason we clerks didn't cancel the tickets for the sure $5 or $10. We held on to them hoping that the lotto luck would rub off on us. Now that's fuzzy logic.

17

The Four Horsemen

Throughout my career at the racetrack, I encountered people who were actually beating the racing game and others who were merely flexing their muscles with minimal results. I identified them as "contenders and pretenders" and kept my eyes on the Rocky Balboas of horseracing. There were plenty more losers than winners, of course, but some of the winners tended to be unforgettable. I encountered some of these winners as I worked on what the racetrack called the "special" windows. These windows were for cashing any bets exceeding 300 to 1, or a minimum of $602, collected on any one gimmick (Daily Double, Exacta, Trifecta, Superfecta, Pick 3, etc.). Lucky gamblers who cashed in at one of these windows had to sign a form and the track then issued them a completed W-2G form to account for their "earnings." A copy was sent to the IRS. Isn't that special.

Between 1984 and 1994, I nicknamed these memorable gamblers the "Four Horsemen." When people hear that term, they tend to think in Biblical terms of the Apocalypse and the forces of human destruction: War, Famine, Conquest, and Death.

Similar to those forces of the Apocalypse, my "horsemen" destroyed my racing world and what I thought I knew about the racing game, all the while making winning look easy. These were the best handicappers around at the time, the cream of the crop.

Larry the Handicapping King

I was working main line three at Arlington Park in 1984, a couple of years after they had closed the tunnel, made famous by Howie in 1979. It was usually slow at that end of the racetrack and I didn't get the big bettors that usually wagered with me in the tunnel. Mostly $2 bettors wandered my way.

One day this twenty-something kid showed up at my window and bet $200 to win on one horse and $200 to win on another in the same race. This got my attention, so I checked the tote board for the odds and I was surprised to see that one horse was 30 to 1 and the other was 25 to 1.

I looked at the racing form and both of these horses looked like they would have trouble finishing the race, let alone winning it. It looked like the new face on the block had a lot of money to blow. When the race went off, I moseyed down to the TV camera to watch it. Turning for home, this kid's picks were running one and two. Middle of the stretch, they were still running one, two. At the wire it was a photo finish between his two horses. Now that's a photo you can only dream about! Do you collect $6,200 or $5,200? You can't call that a bad bet.

After the race I told my co-worker George the story. I described the gambler to him; he didn't know who he was either. We both scanned the crowd, hoping that he'd come back to cash his ticket, then we'd get a better look. But he disappeared like a ghost.

I never saw the mysterious bettor for the rest of the meet. After Arlington closed for the season, I moved over to Hawthorne Racetrack where I worked in the money room. I was running a money room division on the second floor of the clubhouse one afternoon and a friend of mine, Pat, was working a window. I could see that he was bird-dogging one of the customers trying to see what his wagers were. The customer was none other than my ghost from Arlington Park Racetrack.

After the race went off, I asked Pat about the customer he was so closely following. He told me his name was Larry and that he was the best handicapper around. Rumor had it that Larry made more than $600,000 gambling in the previous year. Two years before that, he was only a $10 bettor.

"How did he make the jump from betting $10 to wagering $200 on a horse?" I asked.

"Beats me," Pat replied, "But that's what I'm trying to find out."

Later that day in the money room I received a telephone call (the only phones were behind the lines) from the mutuel manager, who requested Pat's presence in his office after the last race of the day. Nobody liked to be summoned into the office and Pat dreaded going.

I didn't see Pat again until the next night at Maywood Park. Pat was told in no uncertain terms to quit following Larry around and touting his handicapped numbers. It was the first case I knew of a customer seeking a restraining order against a clerk! The customer was always right, especially if he was a big gambler. And during his reign, Larry was the "Handicapping King."

The Nerds

At Sportsman Park I usually worked in the money room, but on Derby Day (the first Saturday in May) we all had to sell at a window. After the second race, one of the clerks, Jeff, eagerly wanted to know what horses my last three customers had just bet on. I told him that I hadn't paid attention.

Jeff looked at me like I was nuts: "Do you know who those guys are?"

"No idea," I replied.

He told me that the last three guys who had bet with me were some of the sharpest handicappers around. They could have fooled me. They looked like a trio of nerds, complete with pocket protectors, glasses, and long greasy hair. According to Jeff, they were computer whizzes using their skill for handicapping horses. Jeff then told me that whenever any of the three came to my window, I should pay close attention to their wagers, and that I just might want to get a bet for myself. My computer knowledge at that time revolved around playing simple PC games, but now I was intrigued.

Throughout that day these three guys bet off and on at my window, and they seemed to cash every race. Jeff was running back and forth to get the numbers from me. I tried to remember the Exactas and Trifectas that they had bet. The problem was that they spent a lot of money in each race and most of the time we couldn't isolate the one particular horse on which to make a straight wager. I chose not to try to mimic their bets, mostly because I didn't have the bankroll.

In 1989, when Arlington Park reopened, I worked at their new intertrack wagering facility after the live meet had closed. The Nerds showed up on opening day. They must have lived in the suburbs and chosen not to travel into the city to wager. While working the IRS window I got to see a lot of them and decided to try to cash in on their handicapping knowledge.

I brought enough cash one day in an attempt to mimic their bets for nine races. We were simulcasting (televising and betting on) races from Hawthorne Racetrack in Stickney, Illinois. It was raining and the track was a sea of mud. I had no idea that handicapping for an off track (wet) was completely different than that for a fast track.

Unfortunately, the Nerds didn't possess that knowledge either. They blanked out for the card. They didn't cash one ticket that day and neither did I! Apparently, I could have done better throwing darts at a board. The lesson I learned on that day goes back to that old saying: "right church, wrong pew." I had the right idea but picked the wrong day to try it out. However, everyone was becoming aware of a link between computers and handicapping.

Computer Frank

Although the Nerds were the first group of gamblers that I knew of who used computers to aid in their handicapping, they weren't the best. That distinction went to a short gambler with black glasses that everyone called "Computer Frank." Just as a new sheriff came to Dodge City every couple of years, Computer Frank showed up one day at Trackside. The way to tell if a big gambler is the real deal is not by how much he bets. I have taken thousand-dollar bets from people who couldn't pick their nose. The Real McCoys will cash big and cash often. Frank could have been Walter Brennan's long lost son.

The following spring Computer Frank had one of the best single days that I have ever witnessed at the racetrack. It was Derby Day and he bet at my window all day long. I don't remember him missing a race and by the day's end he collected more than $100,000—all in cash. He refused to take a personal check or vouchers (which were as good as cash). He wanted all $100 bills and the money room was running low. They had to send someone over to the main money room safe to get the extra $100s.

As he walked out the door that day, I remember thinking that his pants were practically falling down around his ankles from all the money he had stuffed into his pockets. Frank didn't even request a security guard to escort him to his car. He probably didn't want to tip the standard $20 security fee. I'm really surprised he got to his car without somebody hitting him over the head and grabbing that cash. I never got a chance to really know Computer Frank, but I have awe and respect for his ability to have a $100,000 day in the plus column.

Laz

Arlington Park opened the following week and I was off the windows and back to working in the audit department for the summer. It was a nice change of pace to get away from the customers for a while. Arlington ran from May until October, so it was a long break.

After Arlington's thoroughbred meet closed it was back to the windows at Trackside. Computer Frank had vanished, Larry was hit or miss, and even the Nerds made themselves scarce. Who would be the new sheriff? I wondered. It didn't take long for the fastest gun in the Midwest to show up at my window. He was called "Laz" and he was rumored to be an ex-options trader. Standing in the pits had taken its toll on his back and he was trying a new venture.

I regularly worked the information window at Trackside and I cashed most of Laz's big winners, since he had to sign for them. I got to know him a little and we would talk about the stock market; I was interested in his opinion. Of all the gamblers I had come across, he was the most consistent. He cashed at all the different tracks, all the time. Some guys, especially the Nerds, were great at Hawthorne and Sportsman. Larry excelled at Arlington. Laz was all-around consistent and seemed to have the ability to cash at all the local racetracks.

After 1995 I didn't have to work the windows and was full-time in the mutuel office. I lost track of all the big bettors, except Laz. He would call the office every March before taxes were due and ask for a printout of all the big bets for which he had signed.

Laz was a professional gambler and ran his business that way, reporting all his wins and losses. One year I printed out his list of signers (W-2Gs) that was four pages long! I would handicap that as an amazing year.

In my mind, Laz will always be one of the dominant figures in handicapping. Besides his knowledge of racing, he appeared to never let it get emotional. A photo finish seemed to be nothing more to him than part of the business process. It wasn't something that gave him "agita" or high blood pressure, like a lot of gamblers, myself included.

18

Lotteries, Boats, and Indians

At the beginning of the twentieth century, most forms of gambling, such as lotteries and sweepstakes, were illegal in many countries, including the United States. In the 1960s, casinos and lotteries crept back in as a means to raise revenue in addition to taxes. Lotteries are most often run by state or local governments and have been called a regressive tax, played mostly by those hoping for that big "payday," often failing to see that the game is a bad bet. The average lottery ticket pays about 50 cents on the dollar with the operators guaranteeing themselves a healthy profit. If one is lucky enough to win and ends up splitting the prize, he may receive only 30 cents on the dollar after taxes.

Prior to the 1960s, the now-named lottery was called "policy" and was very popular in various ethnic communities, generally attracting low income and working class bettors who usually bet small amounts of money. The payoffs seemed substantial at around 600 to 1, but the true odds were closer to 1,000 to 1. Two nice features were the ability to wager with a bookie, who was more than happy to extend credit, and the absence of income tax on the winnings.

Picking the numbers randomly was a problem back then, leading to rigged games. Using the last three numbers of the published daily balance of the U.S. Treasury supposedly solved that problem. When the Treasury began rounding off that number, the bookies started using the last dollar digit of the daily total handle of win, place and show bets at the local racetrack (how ironic).

The Illinois Lottery started in 1974 (two years before I began my career at the racetrack) and was sold to the public as a means of increasing funding for public education. Through 2007 the lottery had grossed $37 billion and gave $620 million to education in that year alone.

The Illinois lottery claims to be one of the most cost-efficient and profitable lotteries in the world. They've contributed around $14.1 billion to education over its thirty-four-year existence. That may seem impressive, but the annual Illinois Board of Education budget exceeds $9 billion.

According to Ashlee Humphreys, a professor at Northwestern University and a gambling expert, "the discourse that motivates the introduction of a lottery is money for education." But the state takes the money they would have given to education and does something else with it. So the total amount that goes to education is not different but instead comes from the lottery source." This is a modern day bait-and-switch. The one thing that is certain is that every gambling dollar spent on the Illinois Lottery won't be spent on the horses.

Someone once said that a boat is "a hole in the water that you throw money into." I don't think the author of that statement had the riverboat casinos in mind, but it sure seems to apply. In 1990, the Riverboat Gambling Act legalized riverboat gambling in Illinois and the Empress in Joliet was the first riverboat casino to open in the state. Like the lottery, the act passed as a new source of revenue for education.

Riverboat casinos were considered acceptable in Illinois because in theory they imposed limits on gambling. Then-governor Jim Edgar insisted that the casinos go on boats that limited the gambling to three-hour cruise periods. That did not address the situation of a patron who gets off the boat and then on again. A gambler could do this all night or until he ran out of money, whichever came first.

The original tax rate for floating casinos was low because the regulators were unsure of the public's response to the new venture. As the demand began to exceed the supply, more riverboats were opened. All in all there were ten riverboat licenses issued with nine eventually opening. The tenth license was originally scheduled for the suburb of Rosemont, but with rumors of criminal ties to the mayor of that city and other problems, the issuing of the last license has dragged on for over ten years. As the gambling cruise concept took hold, the racetracks in the Chicago suburbs were negatively impacted with dwindling attendance and sinking revenues.

The original theory—that the riverboats would create new local jobs, encourage new commerce, and bring in an abundance of new patrons with money to spend—may have been overly optimistic. The towns with these riverboats may have been financially revived, but I think that most of the boat customers spend their money only on the boats. Its pretty much park, gamble, and leave. There doesn't seem to be a significant increase in outside spending in local businesses. It is true that in 2005, $105 million a year was collected in local taxes that did support community development projects.

The early riverboat casinos charged an admission fee, and the boats had to actually cruise down a river and back. If patrons arrived between cruises, they had to wait for the boat to return and those on the boat had to stay aboard until it docked. Not only were gamblers being held hostage, the idea of paying money to lose money always seemed disturbing. It has been said that one disgruntled loser actually jumped off a riverboat and swam to shore.

The original boats were smoky. This was before second hand smoke was a hot-button issue and laws generated smoking bans. Also, there never seemed to be enough slot machines or gaming table choices. (In the old days it was just gambling, now it's called *gaming*, a more politically correct word.) Patrons were forced to grab any slot machine that was open and stick with it for fear of not finding another in the allotted gaming time. With a small number of tables, people ended up playing blackjack at a $25 minimum bet, if they could find a seat.

The boats were draining off part of the gamblers' bankrolls. I knew many gamblers who, after having a good day at the track, would be off to the boats to throw their winnings into that hole in the water. It got to the point where the owner of Arlington Park considered building a moat with a docked riverboat in the racetrack's infield. He never got that plan passed, as the city of Arlington Heights never qualified as an impoverished area in need of additional tax dollars to help rebuild and rejuvenate.

I was never a fan of the riverboats. I have probably gambled on a boat fewer than six times in my whole life, and two of those trips were made out of respect for someone I had previously worked for in the horseracing industry. My old boss Tom runs the Casino Queen, a riverboat in East St. Louis, and we would visit him from time to time. He was always a generous host on our visits and we felt that donating a little something to the bottom line was appropriate. After our second visit, he told us that it wasn't necessary to go on the boat and gamble. He quipped that our $50 donation wasn't going to make or break any revenue goals or ruin his bonus.

Riverboats have taken a good portion of business away from horseracing, but they must keep improving to keep their customer base happy. Keeping the boats docked to let customers come and go as they please was a huge step in the right direction. Dropping the admission fee was a no-brainer. Try to convince me that they didn't end up with that money anyway. Some boats have even proposed simulcasting horse races for a full evening of entertainment.

In 1988, Congress enacted the Indian Gaming Regulatory Act (IGRA), setting the terms for Native American tribes to operate casinos and bingo parlors. I've read that in the first year the Indian gaming industry produced revenues of nearly $100 million. In 2006, that figure exceeded $25 billion! Various Native American tribes operate over four hundred facilities nationwide.

It's documented that Nevada casinos produced revenues of only $12.6 billion in 2006. Adding in revenue from restaurants, hotels, and entertainment, Nevada casinos doubled their revenues to $24 billion, more closely approaching the revenue of casinos operated by Native American tribes. The Indian casinos put up those numbers without the benefit of sports betting, horseracing, and most table games.

The first Indian casino I entered was in Florida in 2002. We were visiting my Aunt Isabel and Uncle Will in Bonita Springs and they suggested that we go to the casino in a little town called Immokalee, located in the swamps. The casino was running a Texas Holdem poker tournament that evening and the buy-in was $65.

With a new interest in poker by younger gamblers, the tournament format was a lure hard to resist. For $65 players received $2,000 in chips. If they went broke, they could buy another $1,000 in chips for $20. That particular tournament's rules allowed for unlimited re-buys during the first sixty hands played, and they would deal ten more hands to determine who would get to the final table. This format made the play extremely loose and the re-buys were ridiculous. A veteran player wouldn't have recognized the game.

After I busted out, I went to find the rest of the crew that apparently had been skewered by the unforgiving slots. As we emerged from the swamp to start the trek home, I wondered if I'd ever visit another Indian casino again. Back in Illinois, I had managed to avoid them while my co-workers made frequent trips to Wisconsin, even though no one ever seemed to win. The slots were tighter than a wetsuit on a diver.

It took a couple of years, but when we moved to Tucson in 2005, I started playing Holdem again in the local Indian casinos. For gamblers in Tucson, the options are slim. There's dog racing (which I just never considered as a betting sport) and off-track betting; live horseracing is just about dead in this area. The only other options are the various Indian casinos.

Unlike the Florida casino we visited, Tucson Indian casinos are attempting to give Las Vegas casinos a run for their money. Why travel seven or eight hours when there are restaurants, entertainment, and gambling right in the neighborhood? Tucson has delved deeply into the Holdem tournament play in the casinos and also with free poker clubs. Everyone is promising that elusive seat at the World Series of Poker. Las Vegas is still king as far as gambling options available. However, the Indian casinos have taken a bigger bite out of the gaming cake than people could have imagined. The Texas Holdem craze has provided the lucrative tournament format and the increasing number of sites is making Indian casinos the new sheriff in town.

When my Uncle Dick started booking horses in the early 1950s, horseracing was the biggest game in town. The gambling industry now constantly tries to reinvent itself to draw new and younger gamers to the tracks. With the coming-of-age of the instant gratification generation, horseracing, with twenty minutes between races, was doomed to lose the new players.

Simulcasting other tracks between races has been an attempt to fill that gap. Unfortunately, the beauty and power of the racehorse, the finesse and daring of the jockeys, and the ability to handicap a race card appear to be lost on the younger generation.

Prior to 1974 horseracing comprised 100% of the gaming revenue of the state of Illinois. By the year 2006 that had dramatically changed, and horseracing now comprises just 1% of the total gaming revenue, with the riverboats contributing 50% and the lottery 49%. It is true that the gaming revenue has exploded during that period, but the meager 1% contributed by the "ponies" surely means that the horseracing industry, like many of the horses I have bet on, can't get out of the gate.

19

World Series of Poker: The New Lotto

My fascination with the World Series of Poker dates back to 1989. That was the year that an upstart named Johnny Chan was going for an unprecedented third title in a row. Up until Chan's run, seasoned gamblers generally won the tournaments. The story on Johnny was that he came to this country in 1968 from China and attended the University of Houston, majoring in restaurant management. He dropped out of college at age twenty-one and moved to Las Vegas. He played poker when he wasn't working as a fry cook and, as he tells it, he got his brains beat in. As Holdem became more popular he mastered the game.

I purchased the 1988 video showing the final table in which Chan defeated a young Erik Seidel. Chan eventually earned eight other World Series of Poker bracelets between 1992 and 2007. Back then there were no pocket cams showing the players' hole cards, so the tapes got doctored after the fact. As the tape was only forty-five minutes long and the final table took hours, they edited out the less compelling hands to keep viewers' interest. It is still done today, and that's why it seems like aces and kings are always getting beat. Heads up they win about 80% of the time, but on TV it looks like they get beat most of the time.

Johnny Chan seemed to be everybody's favorite in the '89 tournament. His play was aggressive and he always seemed to catch the cards he needed. At the final table was a twenty-three-year-old kid from Wisconsin named Phil Hellmuth. His father was a professor at one of the area universities and he had dropped out of college to play poker. It came down to the two of them with Hellmuth's Ace/9 winning the final hand. He won over $700,000, the biggest prize at that time. To put that in perspective, in the 2006 first event, a $1,500 buy-in tournament, the winner received more than $757,000. The 2006 winner of the $10,000 buy-in featured tournament won over $12 million.

Back in 1989 players had to beat about 350 gamblers over a four-day period. Today there are approximately 8,700 entrants who play over a fourteen-day period, with the majority being amateurs and those who fancy themselves poker players, with a sprinkling of movie stars thrown in for good measure. Stamina has become a very important part of the game.

In 1992 I put a vanity plate on my car that read HOLDEM 6. Up until 2000, no one knew what it stood for. When people asked me what it meant and I told them it was a poker game played at the World Series of Poker (WSOP), most had never heard of the game or the WSOP.

Public interest increased with a number of innovations by the WSOP, chiefly, the lipstick or pocket cam, which allowed viewers to see each player's cards. This made the game much more compelling to a TV audience. Watching paint dry would be more interesting than watching one guy raise and another fold without having any idea of what cards they held.

The next genius idea was to show the chance each hand had at winning the pot. The percentage quickly explained the probability of a win from the starting hands to each flop (cards dealt). Pretty soon everybody knew that small pairs were a slight favorite over two higher cards.

The fact that Holdem is played with only two cards makes it very simple to learn, but it's still hard to master. Watching these tournaments, what has always amazed me is why players constantly look back at their cards. How hard is it to memorize two stinking cards? One Internet site reported trying to enter a monkey into the tournament. It would be entertaining and a major headline if a monkey could take down Johnny Chan. I know how embarrassing that can be. I once got beat at Tic-Tac-Toe by a chicken in a cage. It didn't make the news, but my sister-in-law Carolyn will never let me forget it.

After Phil Hellmuth won in 1989, he did a radio interview on some obscure Wisconsin station. A friend of mine, Bob, who lived in Madison, told me about the interview and got me a tape of it. After listening to it a couple of times, the quest was on to someday enter the WSOP and play in the big game.

I went out and bought a computer poker game that simulated play in a WSOP tournament. Its set-up was similar to the real tournament, except that when I busted out I could start all over again. This particular game didn't track my play, so I documented my own results on paper. By 1992, the results indicated that I was ready for my first attempt at the real WSOP.

My wife and I had planned a vacation to California in April to visit her sister Carolyn (the one who sends me chicken paraphernalia). I had a few extra days off so I scheduled a pit stop in Las Vegas on the way home. I had saved $3,500 to play in some satellite tournaments and was willing to give it three tries at winning the $10,000 entry fee for the WSOP.

The one-table $1,000 buy-in was the most popular way to get in. These single table events were over in about two hours, and if you caught some cards early and got lucky, you had a chance. In my first attempt I was so nervous that when I caught three jacks on the flop I spilled all my chips in the pot. You didn't have to be Mike Caro (author of the famous book on reading poker tells) to figure out my hole cards. The other players did and immediately everybody dropped. After finishing fifth out of ten I didn't feel so bad because it was only my first crack at it.

I went downstairs for dinner—the best $5 steak I ever had. Feeling full and refreshed, I went back to my hotel room, had a long pep talk with myself, and then went down for try number two. I fared much better with my second effort and when we got down to three players—myself included—I thought that I had a chance.

But then my cards went dead and the blinds went up, so I was the next to go. I was down $2,140 and had nothing to show for it. I had one more bullet in the chamber if I wanted to fire it. I retreated to my room to contemplate what to do. After much thought, rather than try a third time, I bought six WSOP hats and brought them back for our poker group. I would save the G-note for another day.

When I got back and told the homeboys about the tournament and my bad beat stories, we decided to play some mini-tournaments among ourselves and go as a group to Vegas in two years. By then we'd all have a better feel for the game.

Our plan was to cut money out of each pot every time we played cards for the next two years. In 1994 we had enough for each player to enter one satellite for the $1,500 no-limit tournament. The one-table satellites cost $150 to enter with the winner getting the $1,500 needed to enter the tournament. Whoever got in was playing for the group. We all brought our golf clubs just in case we had some free time.

The six of us signed up for separate satellites so we wouldn't have to compete against one another. Since it was my big idea, I had to go first and I did not set the bar very high, lasting only thirty minutes. That low standard was quickly smashed when Steve sat down and busted out on the second hand with pocket kings. He lit a cigarette one minute (you could smoke at the tables back then) and he was walking away talking to himself the next. Bob was next and fared no better or worse, so we were down to three players. Since the satellites went all day and night, we went to dinner to discuss strategy.

Angelo was next up and we all knew that his wild play would confuse the table. Maybe this is what we needed to change our luck. Angelo sat down and caught cards from the beginning; he either had high pairs or would flop two pair. His chips were piling up and he was having a blast.

As guys busted out, they couldn't believe the hands Angelo was catching. Maybe the rest of us play too close to the vest and wild play is the way to go. Even so, I wanted to jump over the rail and tell Angelo to slow down his play, but what did I know? Two hands later he was gone—the luck ran out. We all had to give him props for lasting the longest so far.

We were down to two bullets in our six-shooter. Bill went next and fired a blank. The whole enchilada was now on Roger's shoulders. We needed someone to actually make it in this tournament and Roger had shown promise in our little faux satellites. As memory serves me, he got down to the final three players when a pair of jacks did him in. He hit three-of-a-kind on the flop and went all in, but one player went to the river to fill his flush. It was a good thing we all brought our golf clubs.

Coincidentally, that was the same hand that proved to be my downfall in the second satellite in 1992. I also had three jacks and lost to a flush, but I lost to a guy named Huck Seed. Well, I never forget a face or a particular hand, so when Huck Seed won the World Series of Poker in 1996, I told my friends that he was the guy who knocked me out in 1992. They said I was nuts, but I know it was him.

My next effort came in 1996 when my mother-in-law took us all to Vegas for her seventieth birthday. How convenient that her birthday was May 3, right at the beginning of the main event WSOP tournament.

We would be there two days before the start of the big show, so I decided to try a super satellite being held at the Gold Coast Casino. The buy-in was $200 and they awarded up to three $10,000 seats to the main event starting on Monday. It was perfect: satellite on Sunday and, if I got in, the tournament started the next day. We were scheduled to stay through Tuesday anyway and if I did well in tournament play I could always change my flight.

There were about 120 players and the action was fast. I was moved and my table broke up three times in the first hour. We were down to sixty players in no time before the action slowed down. With the last move I finally got comfortable and was playing well and accumulating some chips.

My demise came with that dreaded big slick—the nickname for ace/king. The theory is that to win a tournament you have to win with ace/king *and* you also have to beat ace/king. Unfortunately, in that game I only got it half right. For the next four years poker went on the back burner.

In 2000, I could get only four of the usual suspects to go with me back to Vegas. This time positive thinking ruled and the golf clubs stayed home. On this outing it was every man for himself. We targeted the $2,000 no-limit Holdem event with the one-table satellites costing $220. The day before the satellite I got lucky on the horses, so I had the $2,000 to get in if I didn't win the satellite. I would give myself two tries in the satellites before I'd finance my own buy-in.

On my second try I won my entry fee, so I wasn't going home broke if I busted out. They paid us in special chips that I thought were only good for the tournament, so I registered right away. When

Bill won his satellite he discovered we could sell back the chips at a slight loss to a woman who then turned around and sold them for a slight profit to players unwilling to stand in the long lines for their buy-in chips. Bill figured he had his lucky run and took the cash. Even if I had known, I never would have sold my chips. I came to play.

The tournament started at noon the next day with almost four hundred players. The winner was to receive about $350,000; if I made the top forty I'd get paid. Usually about 10% of the players get paid with the lion's share going to the top five. The winner would receive between 35% and 40% of the net pool.

Play wasn't too fast at my table, and by dinnertime, with fewer than one hundred players remaining; I had increased my stack of chips from $2,000 to $8,800. I really felt comfortable at my table and was holding about average with my chip stack. Around 7:30 p.m. they decided to break up tables and we all drew for different seats. I drew a table in the corner, took my $9,000 in chips, and went to my new home where all my competition seemed to be holding at least fifty grand. I was definitely low man.

My strategy was to be conservative and only play quality hands for a round or two. This way I hoped to get a read on some of the players. The table was loose with a lot of raising going on so I could check a good hand and probably get raised behind me and then I could re-raise. Getting heads up with a higher pair would allow me to double up my stack.

The plan was perfect; I was first off the big blind. When I looked down, there they were—two beautiful black aces. I meekly anted and waited for the raise; none came. The best-laid plans often go astray and as I awaited the flop with my quality hand, the dealer turned over 5-5-2 unsuited. This was no time to slow play aces now so I bet $2,000. Four players folded and one raised $2,000 back. I didn't hesitate to go all in and he quickly called. When he flipped over 5-2 for the full house, I couldn't believe it. He called an $800 bet with 5-2 unsuited. I wait seven hours to see my first pair of tournament aces and now I might be going home.

I had only two outs and it didn't look good. This would be a great story if an ace fell on the river to squash his horrible 5-2, but it didn't. The plan was good; the execution was poor. I played cute and got burned. As I made that long walk out of the pit, I stopped to see how many players were left. There were sixty-four still alive, so I was twenty-four off the money. At that moment I didn't care if I ever came back to Vegas or played in another tournament again.

Chris Ferguson won the big event that year and to date he was the last of the known gamblers to win it. It used to be that if there were 300 players in the tournament, 250 were professionals of some sort and 50 were amateurs (or "dead money" as they were called). Today, with around 8,700 players trying for the pie-in-the-sky, probably 7,700 are amateurs. The only chance the pros have is to shear the sheep that get lucky in some side games. Gee, I wonder if that goes on?

With the popularity of today's event, your odds of winning are similar to matching six bouncing lottery balls. I may give it another shot some day, but those black aces not only put out the fire inside me, they turned it to cold wet ash.

20

The Summer of Saratoga

In my thirty years of working at Arlington Park there were two years when it was shut down. After the meet closed in 1997, the owner decided to close down as the competition from the riverboats was straining the horseracing industry. Jobs at the track became scarce. Management had a meeting to set up a new corporate structure and flow charts were passed out.

At that meeting there were about twenty-five remaining employees, and they decided to group everyone in one section of the administrative side of the building. This way it would not look like a ghost town with everyone spread out throughout the track. That was as close to working a regular job as I ever had at the racetrack.

The nice part was that since we weren't racing in 1998, I could actually take a summer vacation like other normal people did. My sister Mari-Jo and her husband Jimmy wanted to go to Saratoga Racetrack in New York. My wife and I joined them on the trip during the second week in August.

Saratoga Racetrack is located in upstate New York, outside of Albany, in the little town of Saratoga Springs. The mineral springs were frequented by the likes of Daniel Webster, Martin Van Buren, Washington Irving, Andrew Jackson, and Franklin Pierce. Later came the Vanderbilts, Whitneys, Rockefellers, and the J.P. Morgans.

With the arrival of the wealthy and the influential, horseracing naturally followed. Saratoga Raceway opened in 1863 and is the oldest thoroughbred track in the country. One of the greatest thoroughbreds of all time, Man o' War, suffered his only defeat in 1919 at Saratoga. He finished second to a horse appropriately named Upset.

Some gamblers today call Saratoga "the graveyard of the chalk" because the favorites seem to get beat more often than not. I don't know if that's statistically true, but it makes for a good legend.

We were scheduled to arrive in Saratoga Springs on a Thursday afternoon so that we could spend Friday and Saturday at the track, then return home on Sunday. Early on Thursday I downloaded Friday's racing card to study on the plane so that I would be well prepared for betting the next day.

I made sure that I had an extra $128 to play the Pick 6 on Friday's last six races. That amount would allow me two horses in each race and the pools were usually large at this meet. Even without a carryover, a single winner might receive more than $50,000.

As I studied the racing card I felt good about the last six races. By Friday morning I had my two selections in each race written down, ready for the Pick 6. All I had to do was walk in the track, make a beeline for the first open teller window, make my bet and lock up the ticket. If only my life were so simple.

The drive from our hotel in Albany to Saratoga took about thirty minutes. Following the signs to the racetrack, we parked in a huge forest preserve. We followed the crowd and out of nowhere appeared this majestic sight. The grand old lady of racetracks stood out in a large clearing. I was just as excited as the first time I saw Arlington Park as a kid.

We went directly to the will-call window to pick up our passes and box seats for the two days. That was one of the perks I received from working at a racetrack. Someone can always get you passes and box seats at another track. Call it a professional courtesy.

Being untouched by time is how a racetrack should be, and Saratoga was just that. It was how I remembered old Arlington Park, but even better. It appeared that the only upgrade ever made at Saratoga was the installation of escalators. There was no dining room, no indoor seating, and no air conditioning.

The paddock area was truly out of the 1800s. Twelve trees had numbers nailed on them, each representing a horse in the upcoming race. Ten minutes prior to each race the horses were saddled under the shade of the trees and then paraded out to the track. I've seen many a paddock area and most are very generic, but I will always remember Saratoga's. The rest of the grounds were like an old country fair. Food stands, souvenir shops, and people settled in lawn chairs facing televisions strapped high into the trees.

We eventually found our box seats—outside! There were ceiling fans to keep us cool in the August heat. We got down to handicapping the first race and since the Pick 6 didn't start until the fourth race I decided to wait to make my wager. If I got lucky in the first three races I could add a horse or two to my Pick 6 selections.

After three losers in a row, I was looking for partners for my Pick 6. With partners, however, comes new input. That ticket I'd worked on the night before never saw the light of day. In the first two races of the Pick 6 we substituted two new horses for two of my original choices. Those who see a pattern here will figure out which horses won races 4 and 5: the two that we eliminated. We had the winners in races 6, 7, 8, and 9, but unfortunately four out of six gets you nadda, zippo, zilch, and zero.

The really bad news: No one had all six winners. Any tickets with five out of six paid $1,500 and the remaining pool of $55,000 rolled over until the next day. What that also means is that the original numbers I had written down were worth the whole pool! One winner—me—could have collected $55,000 pretax. So much for partners.

There was some good that came out of my handicapping on those last six races. Being out of the Pick 6 after races 4 and 5, we decided to play the Pick 3 in races 6, 7, and 8. We had those winners and split up a nice Pick 3 between the four of us, although we had a bit of controversy along the way.

Going into the eighth race we needed a horse named Flo's Best to win in order to collect on our Pick 3. The horse was the favorite just like our own Aunt Flo. My brother-in-law Jimmy got up to make a bet and I asked him which horse he was betting on. "Flo's Best," he answered. When I told him that it's bad luck to bet on a horse that we already had in the Pick 3, he looked at me like I was nuts. We argued right up until post time and finally he gave up and sat down. The three guys behind us were laughing hysterically, but I think they agreed with me.

After Flo's Best won we collected our big Pick 3. Jimmy gave me a dirty look, but I assured him that if he had made that extra bet the horse would have lost. He just had to take one for the team.

We were all winners that day, but it could have been a tremendous day. Of course the next day, Saturday, was a different story. We put more money into the Pick 6, as the pool was twice Friday's amount, but we didn't come close. In fact I don't think that I cashed a ticket all day. On Sunday's plane ride home I vowed that someday I'd catch a Pick 6 at Saratoga.

We are hoping to be back to Saratoga in the future. With a little luck maybe I can turn the tide on history repeating itself.

21

Starnet and Internet Gambling

As the fall of 1998 crept in, the summer of Saratoga became a distant memory. I could put my Pick 6 dreams on hold until next July. The stock market was heating up and that was all anybody talked about. It seemed everybody was making money and small stocks were all the rage. Stock sites like Raging Bull were getting thousands of hits a day on bulletin board stocks.

In the old days these stocks were called pink sheet stocks because their prices were not available in the papers, only on the pink sheets. With the advent of the Internet anyone could get quotes and buy and sell shares of these stocks all day. Most sold for under $1 and didn't have any analysts covering them. This made them very risky and easily manipulated by hype and hearsay. At the time, I was mostly in mutual funds, but had a few stocks in one of my retirement accounts.

Around Thanksgiving of that year, my co-worker Jack and I were discussing the markets. He was talking up a small stock called Starnet that he recently purchased. As my Uncle Dick the bookmaker always said when someone gave him a hot horse, "Give me the story."

It seemed that our simulcast coordinator, Brant, was working with a small Internet company that had proprietary software for gambling on the Web. At that point Internet gambling was in its infancy and this company had the first software package available to handle the bets. To make things even better, Arlington Park was considering putting horseracing on the Web and possibly partnering with Starnet.

The stock was selling for 84 cents a share. I normally didn't get involved with these so-called penny stocks, but I decided to take a flyer and buy some shares. I had $3,500 in cash in one of my IRA accounts, so I bought 4,000 shares for a total investment of $3,360 plus commissions. I figured that was all I could lose if the stock went to zero. Since my broker didn't handle pink sheet stocks over the Internet, I had to call in to make the purchase; to sell would require the same procedure.

Two weeks after I purchased Starnet, it was trading at 50 cents a share. Here we go again, another dog with fleas, I thought. In late January 1999, the stock market was roaring and Starnet started to move. It went from 50 cents a share to more than $4 in three weeks. I was tempted to take some profits, but decided to hold tight.

It traded sideways for a month and then exploded to more than $16 a share in April. I would track the stock on the Raging Bull website and it alone was getting some three thousand hits a day. Rumors abounded about the stock splitting and different partnerships forming.

At this point, Arlington was no longer rumored to be interested in any partnering with Starnet. Arlington had found out that Starnet had originally started as a porn site and still received income from that venue. They didn't want any part of that and wanted them to sell off that portion of their business. Starnet didn't want to lose its sure moneymaker (porn), so Arlington dropped out of the mix and the stock dropped to about $8 in May.

Brant was leaving Arlington and going to work for Starnet full-time. He told Jack and me not to worry; the stock was going back up. I gave him my home phone number and told him to keep in touch and call if the company prospects started to deteriorate.

In June the stock started to move again and by mid-July it was in the $20s. Rumors were running rampant about a 2/1 stock split. At $20 a share I had turned $3,360 into more than $80,000 in seven months, on paper. On top of it all Saratoga was opening its meet that week and I had a date with the Pick 6. My idea was to watch and track the first two weeks at Saratoga and then go after the Pick 6.

On July 30, Starnet opened up at $30 a share. I was sitting on $120,000 and I thought about selling at least half. Raging Bull's site got over eight thousand hits that day and the talk was all about the stock splitting 2/1. You never want to sell a stock before it splits because usually the price pops up right after. They called these stocks *split runners* because after they split, they run up and then split again. A lot of stocks that split in the late 1990s followed this pattern. At the time we were in the biggest market bubble in history and everybody was making too much money to sell. Unfortunately, those paper profits wouldn't be realized until investors cashed in.

Starnet never announced the split that day and the stock closed down at $23. Now I was ready to sell at least half when it got back to $30 again. Well, that never happened and the stock then dropped under $20 to a final close of $16 a share.

There went $56,000 in about a week. I was burning through paper profits faster than a sailor in a whorehouse with six months' pay in his pockets. I promised myself that I'd get out at $20 and the stock immediately went down to $12. I put my foot down and declared that the minute it hit $16, I was getting out.

On Friday morning I was watching the stock trading at about $14 a share. The night before I had downloaded the Saratoga card and was going to make my first Pick 6 ticket of the meet. The card looked good and I had dreams of capturing that $55,000 that had eluded me last summer.

There would be no distractions this time. I was going to go to Trackside, the off-track betting establishment, at noon to make the bet and then come home. All I had left to do was to go online and get the scratches for the card. Ten minutes online was all I needed.

In 1999 there was no cable modem or DSL in my town. We had a dial-up modem that used the phone line. After getting the scratches and checking their weather, I left my house for Trackside. It took twenty minutes to get there, ten minutes to make my Pick 6, and twenty minutes back. I was gone fifty minutes, tops. When I got back I had a voice message from Brant: "Jim, call me immediately," and he left a number.

I called him back and he asked, "Where were you? I tried to get a hold of you an hour ago and your line was busy." What were the odds of Brant calling me in that particular ten-minute time frame when I was on the computer? Apparently better than one would think.

He told me to turn on the business channel and check out the story on Starnet. Both the president and CEO were taken out of their offices in handcuffs and the company was being charged with pornography. The stock was plummeting and was down to $4, with the possibility that trading on it might be halted for the day.

If I had gotten Brant's first call, I might have been able to get out at $14 a share on the Starnet stock. Instead, there went another $40,000 down the drain. In one week I lost $96,000 on paper. If I was that sailor, I could've bought the whorehouse! The stock kept on trading that day and I was able to sell 1,500 shares at $5.50 for $8,250. Two weeks later I sold 500 more shares at $4 and decided to keep the last 2,000 shares.

I rationalized to myself that turning $3,400 into $10,200 in 9 months was not that bad of an investment. Deep down inside I knew that I had let about $100,000 in paper profits disappear: $60,000 because I was greedy and $40,000 because I picked the wrong day to make a Pick 6 ticket. The last 2,000 shares I finally let go at 64 cents, which was 20 cents less than what I had originally paid.

The stock stopped trading in 2002, but I kept a copy of the chart pattern on Starnet from 1998 till its demise. The stock took a ride from 50 cents to $30 back to 20 cents, which was the last quote I got. This was similar to a lot of stock charts leading up to the bursting of the bubble in 2000. They all had that elevator ride up and down, some more dramatically than others.

What was amazing about Starnet was that it went from a low of a half a buck to a high of $30, which is a "60 bagger" in market terms. You don't see a lot of those moves or have a chance to participate in them. Since I'll probably never be involved in one of them again in my lifetime, anything I learned here is a moot point.

22

On Any Given Sunday (or Monday)

Of all the football games on television, probably the one most wagered on is Monday Night Football. It's "get-even time" for those who owe their bookies from the weekend, which is the majority of gamblers. For those lucky enough to be ahead, it's extra icing on the cake.

The National Football League makes a valiant attempt to put good games on Monday night, but it hasn't always worked out because the games are scheduled so far in advance. The preceding season's winners sometimes turn out to be the current season's losers. Also, injuries to players can take any team out of contention early.

Some teams have consistently performed well on Monday nights (see Oakland Raiders), while others were horrible (see Chicago Bears). If I had to speculate, I would imagine that the Monday night football game took its toll on gamblers, putting the losers farther in the hole and taking away some of the winners' profits.

A friend of mine told me about a different type of football pool that he had played in. It cost $100 per entry and all you had to do was pick one team to win to advance to the next week. Your team didn't have to beat the spread; all they had to do was win the game straight up. The same team could be used over and over again, so it was easy to ride a hot team most of the year. It sounded pretty simple to me, so I got in with my buddy Bob and my brother Jerry.

We lasted about four weeks, until one of the heavily favored teams that we picked was upset. Not as easy as I thought! With two thousand people in the pool that year, the payoff was large—$200,000—with the winners splitting up the total for a take of about $30,000 apiece. The rules allowed splits if all agreed and when there were less than 1% of the entries remaining. In a pool the size of two thousand, that would be twenty people or fewer.

The next year Bob and I got into the pool again. Learning from past experience, the two things that we were going to avoid were Monday night games and teams playing on the road. The strategy worked well through week eleven. It seemed that most of the big chalks (teams favored by more than 10 points) got upset when not at home. The problem was that sometimes those were the only playable teams, and week twelve of the season was one of those weeks.

The Green Bay Packers were on the road playing the Indianapolis Colts. Quarterback Brett Favre was in his prime and the Packers had just won the Super Bowl the previous year. This was a pre-Payton Manning Indy team that was terrible. They had lost their first ten games and their first—and second-string quarterbacks were both hurt. The bookmakers had the Colts as 17-point underdogs at home. Green Bay would easily score 30 to 40 points; Indy would have trouble-scoring 10.

Although it was an away game, it looked like the cinch of the week. We decided to go against our strategy of not betting on teams playing on the road who were large favorites. The Colts' third-string quarterback couldn't possibly outscore Brett Favre and the Packers.

The Packers didn't disappoint and rolled up 38 points. Unfortunately, the hapless Colts scored 41 and came away with the win, knocking Bob and me out of the pool. To put that in perspective, Green Bay went on to win the last five regular season games giving up a total of only 65 points (that's 13 points per game). They won both post-season games and went on to the Super Bowl, only to lose to the Denver Broncos.

I took a couple of years off from the pool and in 2001 decided to get in with three of my co-workers, Jack, Mark, and Bilko. By that time the pool cost $200 per entry so we put up $50 a piece. We would each pick a team and then brainstorm to narrow them down to a single choice.

With the increased entry fee that year the pool grew to more than $250,000, so when there were thirteen lucky gamblers or fewer (1%) left they could split up the money. There was always the option to play down to winner take all.

The first two weeks the pool was cut in half to six hundred players. After week five, there were fewer than one hundred players left. There wasn't just the expected one upset a week, but three or more. When week six rolled around, we had trouble deciding on a pick. We just couldn't agree and argued back and forth over four different teams, somehow ended up with the Monday night game. The New York Giants (our pick) were at home against the Philadelphia Eagles.

The Giants went to the Super Bowl in 2000 (they lost) and were picked this year as a real contender. On top of that, they owned the Eagles, beating them in the last nine games. As much as I hated Monday night games, this one looked real good.

When we got the breakdown for the week showing how many players chose each team, we saw that there were only seven games selected and we were the only ones who took the Monday night game. We didn't know if that was good or bad, but if there were a few upsets we'd be in good shape.

We got more than our share of upsets, and when the dust settled on Sunday evening there were eight guys left besides us. All we had to do was win our game on Monday night and vote to split up the pool.

At this point a serious sports gambler would hedge his bet. When he is in a position to make money he locks in a profit. The smart thing to do would be to bet a minimum of $800 on the Eagles getting 7 points. If the Giants won, we'd probably split up the pool and lose the $800 plus the juice ($880 total).

If the Eagles won, we'd get $200 each for our trouble. And the icing on the cake would be if the Giants won but didn't cover the spread (7 points); then we'd win both the bet and a piece of the pool.

Of course we didn't cover our butts and all went home to watch the Monday night game like cheerleaders. We weren't worried; after all, the Giants had beaten the Eagles nine straight games.

When the game started, I felt confident. The Giants took the opening drive and went down the field easily. The Eagles defense held and the Giants kicked a field goal. The next time the Giants got the ball they drove down the field and again had to settle for 3 points. The first quarter ended with our team leading 6 to 0.

In the second quarter the Giants kicked another field goal and led 9-0 at the half. They dominated the first half and all they could manage were three field goals. Better than a poke in the eye with a sharp stick, I mused.

The third quarter started with the Giants driving down into Eagle territory, only to be intercepted. They got the ball back, drove again, and missed a field goal. My stomach was now churning. The Eagles had done nothing and were only a touchdown and a field goal away from winning. Meanwhile the Giants had been in scoring position five times and had only 9 points to show for it. One thing I learned about sports: "Never let a team hang around." You have to put them away when you have the chance.

In the middle of the fourth quarter the Eagles finally got on the board with a field goal. The Giants drove down again and their quarterback Kerry Collins threw another interception. The Eagles had the ball with three minutes left. All the Giants had to do was stop them one more time. That was when Donavan McNabb turned into the player he is today. He scrambled around and, avoiding tacklers, drove the Eagles all the way down the field. His touchdown pass with time running out sealed our fate.

The next day at work was like a funeral. Actually, it was only the wake. The funeral came later when we found out that the pool was divided up, with the eight lucky winners getting $31,250 apiece. Divide the pool by nine and our share would have been $27,778 or $6,945 apiece. For the next week we cursed everybody on the Giants, even the water boy.

By that time in my life I'd been through so many bad beats, to me this was just another brick in the wall. The one who took it the hardest was Mark, he couldn't let it go. Even when I retired, five years later, he would still bring up that game and ask me, "How much did that cost us?" I told him that some guys just aren't lucky and have to work for their money. Unfortunately, we're those guys.

23

Bejarano and the Pick 4

Pick 4 wagering had become very popular around 2000. Part of its popularity was due to the fact that racetracks, such as Hollywood, Santa Anita, and Churchill Downs, were guaranteeing that pools would have certain amounts ($100,000 to $250,000). Though not as large as the Pick 6 guarantees (up to $1 million), it's more than acceptable for a wager that gets paid off regularly.

To me, the Pick 4 is the poor man's Pick 6. First off, the Pick 4 is only a $1 wager, allowing the bettor the luxury of spending half the amount normally spent on a Pick 6. Secondly, only four winners are needed instead of six, which cuts the multiples way down.

Two horses in every race of the Pick 6 cost $128, while the same bet in the Pick 4 costs only $16. Adding a horse in each race and the Pick 6 costs $1,458 ([3x3x3x3x3x3] x 2), while that same bet in a Pick 4 costs $81 (3x3x3x3). That's a huge difference.

I know that the average Pick 6 will always pay more than the average Pick 4; that's not the point. What matters is how much of a bettor's bankroll should go into each gimmick bet. The more horses covered in each race, the better the chance of winning. Betting Pick 4s allows the bettor to cover more horses for a lot less money.

If one or two horses can be singled out in two out of the four races in the Pick 4, then it's possible to go deeper (use more horses) in the other two races. Most professionals use this strategy in the Pick 6 to cut down on their costs.

This strategy in a Pick 4 with two solid horses would allow the bettor to buy out the other two races if the fields weren't too long. For example, if the two other races had eight and seven horse fields respectively, then the total cost of the Pick 4 would be $56 (8x7x1x1). All that's needed is for the two single horses to win and, hopefully, long shots in the other two races. This would guarantee a nicely priced Pick 4. If the two single horses were also a decent price, it could be a monster Pick 4.

Now that I've set the table, it's time for the dinner story.

A new jockey had burst onto the scene in the summer of 2002. His name was Rafael Bejarano and he hailed from Peru. He won his first race at River Downs in July of that year.

As with all apprentice jockeys he didn't get many mounts that year. The following year he started to get more, but was still not widely followed. As he rode mostly on the Kentucky circuit (Churchill, Keeneland, and Turfway), I had never heard of him. That all changed in March 2004.

Keith, who worked for the racing board, was a big Bejarano fan, having followed him from the start. Every day he would wander into my office with the latest Bejarano update: "Rafael wins another race and pays $34.80. I can't believe that they haven't bet him down," he would say. Keith firmly believed that Bejarano could win riding a mule.

On March 12, at Turfway Park in Kentucky, Rafael won seven out of nine races on the card, and they weren't all favorites. The next day he came back with five out of nine—twelve wins in two consecutive days! Some jockeys don't win that many races in a month. Keith was beside himself; he had found the pot of gold at the end of the rainbow, but couldn't cash in.

As a state employee he wasn't allowed to bet on horseracing in the state of Illinois, even on his day off. He occasionally drove up to Dairyland, the dog track in Wisconsin, and wagered when he wasn't working. Keith and Dan were probably the only two state employees I knew who actually followed those rules.

Bejarano won the riding title at Turfway Park with 196 wins, moved on to Keeneland, and finally Churchill Downs in May. June arrived and he was still winning with big prices. Keith informed me of most winners and the mutuel payouts.

On the third Saturday in June I asked my boss if I could come in early and leave at 1:00 p.m. This was something I rarely did, but my wife and I had been invited to Val's fiftieth birthday party at her cottage. A friend of my sister Mari-Jo, I'd also known Val a long time. We'd never been able to accept an invitation to the lake house she and Jim owned due to my working weekends at the track.

This particular time I would live like normal people who had their weekends free. After twenty-eight years of working Saturdays and Sundays in the summer, I figured I deserved it. With that in mind I got up early that fine Saturday morning. It was going to be a perfect afternoon to spend on the boat at Val's lake house. Getting to work by 7:00 a.m., I had my three computers up and running by 7:30. By noon I was almost finished and would be out of work within the hour, pick up my wife, and be at the party by 2:30. A fun-filled weekend day awaited us.

About 12:15 p.m., Keith walked into my office with the racing program in his hand. He asked if I had seen the Churchill card for that day. I really had been too busy to look, so I asked him, "What's up?" He proceeded to tell me that Bejarano was riding in two stake races that day. Those races were part of the guaranteed $500,000 Pick 4. On top of that, his odds were 30 to 1 in one race and 15 to 1 in the other.

He handed me the program and I looked at Bejarano's mounts in those two races. The horses had pretty good form to be going off at those odds. I told him that they would probably get bet down. He responded that the public refuses to bet Bejarano's horses down, so they'll be big prices. I looked at the other two races that were part of the Pick 4. One had seven horses and the other race had eight. Those races looked pretty wide open to me. Anybody had a chance to win.

I remember to this day the exact words that I said to Keith: "For $56 we could go Bejarano, all, all, Bejarano" as he was riding in the first and fourth leg of the Pick 4. That would cost us $28 apiece, if we were to split the bet. I asked Keith what the chances were of him winning two races at those boxcar odds? He proclaimed that he'd seen him win with lesser horses.

Knowing that Keith couldn't make a wager, I got the feeling that he was waiting for me to say, "I'll make the bet, let's go partners." I wasn't supposed to bet either, but it would be safe to say that there wasn't one person in the history of the mutuel department who had not wagered at some time while working at the racetrack.

I looked at the clock and it was 12:30. I told Keith that I had to go somewhere and was leaving in thirty minutes. He put his head down and left my office. I knew that he would never make the bet himself.

I turned on my office TV and found the channel showing the races at Churchill Downs. The fourth race was going off and the track was sloppy. It looked like it had been raining all morning and wasn't going to let up.

A couple of things that I have learned during my illustrious horseracing career about sloppy or muddy tracks: (1) you can get big priced horses because of the track condition, and (2) lesser or newer jockeys will ride harder on a bad track. The old timers and good jockeys can be tentative, as the track conditions can cause spills. Rafael Bejarano would ride and win on any track.

Knowledge is only good when put to use. I'm sure that someone has coined that phrase. If not, I am doing it now and taking credit for it. We had the knowledge that the hottest rider in the country was being overlooked in the betting in two stake races. He was riding on a track that might just favor long shots. Finally, for $56 we could make a wager that could pay much more than betting both of his horses to win.

Knowing all of this I left work as scheduled, not making the bet. I got home, changed, and was out the door in ten minutes.

We no sooner got on the road and my cell phone rang. It was Keith. He had never called my cell before. The number was posted on the wall to be used only in case of an emergency.

"Anything wrong?" I asked, thinking that there was a tote problem at work.

"Bejarano just won the first leg of the Pick 4 and paid $43," he replied.

Immediately my mind went into overdrive. Had we made the bet we would have been live to the last race of the Pick 4, having all the horses in the next two races. I calmed myself down by recalling all the doubles and Pick 3s I've had going into the last leg over the years and not cashing the ticket. One time at Sportsman Park I had six out of ten horses in the second half of a Daily Double and still missed cashing the double. I rationalized that Bejaranos mount (our single pick) at 30 to 1 would never win the last race. After all, it was the feature race and there were a lot of good horses entered. I told Keith, "He can't possibly win that last race."

"I hope you're right," Keith said dejectedly.

For the next hour or so of driving I turned up the music and tried to forget about horseracing. Whenever my mind wandered back to the last race, I kept repeating over and over to myself, "He won't win the race." That turned into "He can't win the race." And finally, "God, please don't let him win this race."

We were about five miles from Val's cottage and I had finally rid my mind of horseracing. When my cell phone rang my only thought was, "anybody but Keith."

It was Keith.

"Jim, you won't believe it; Bejarano just won the feature race."

"What did the horse pay?" I asked.

"I hope you're sitting down, because he paid $105 to win," he replied.

I didn't want to ask Keith the next question, but knew that I had to. "What did the Pick 4 pay?" There was silence for a moment and then the news just got worse; the answer was "more than $100,000."

The only thing left to do now was to put the final nail in the coffin and find out approximately how much this non-wager cost us. I knew that Keith would know how many winning tickets were sold on the Pick 4, so I asked him. He told me that there were six winners nationwide so the net pool was about $600,000. Divide that by seven winners (the original six plus our phantom ticket), and the payoff drops down to a mere $85,000.

I figured that I had two choices that evening: (1) block out what had happened and have a good time with my two-legged friends, or (2) go jump in the lake on account of my four-legged friends. I think that I made the right choice and stayed in dry dock.

Rafael Bejarano went on to win 455 races that year earning him the North American Jockey title. Out of all of those races, there were only two that I cared about.

Since that day I have not cashed more than a handful of winning tickets betting on Bejarano and none of those were long shots. He is my Jonah, losing when I bet on him and winning when I bet against him. I know that will never change. I had my chance once and I blew it.

The gambling gods had the last laugh. Apparently, just like the golf gods, the gambling gods don't allow a mulligan. No second chance for me.

24

Great Scam, Poor Plan

Weather wise, October is a Jekyll-and-Hyde month in Chicago—it could get to seventy degrees or it might snow, sometimes both in the same day! The last week of October 2002 began typically in that regard: rain, wind, and cold. By Friday, everyone at Arlington Park Racetrack was in a panic. They were finally hosting their first Breeders' Cup Championship and *Mother Nature* was not cooperating. Getting good weather in late October was dicey at best.

The current owner, Dick Duchossois (Mr. D) had pulled a rabbit out of his hat back in 1985 after the grandstand burned down. In two weeks he cleared the rubble, constructed temporary grandstands, and ran the Arlington Million. Not a small feat even by his standards. The new Arlington that emerged over the next three years was like no other racetrack in the country. From the European type paddock and luxury suites, down to the grandstand area, it was exquisite. But not even Mr. D could control the weather.

By Breeders' Cup Saturday, the best the weathermen could do was fifty degrees and no rain. Still, a sold-out crowd of 46,118 showed up for one of horseracing's most important days (the Kentucky Derby being the other).

When Arlington reopened in 1989, it was set up to accommodate between 30,000 and 35,000 customers. For the Breeders' Cup, temporary grandstands were erected on both turns of the track for the overflow crowd. There were wall-to-wall bettors and the mutuel lines were long. I remember walking through the mass of bodies and thinking that in the thirteen years since we had reopened I'd never seen so many people at the track. I didn't know it at that time, but this was probably the pinnacle of Chicago racing.

There were eight Breeders' Cup races that day, with $13 million in purse money. The last race was called the Classic and it carried a $4 million purse (the pool of money to be distributed to the first five horses in the race), of which 60% went to the winner.

The Classic was also the last race of the Ultra Pick 6 where they expected between $2 and $3 million in the pool to be paid to those bettors who were able to select six winners in the six consecutive designated races. Breeders' Cup days were known for good-priced horses, so the Pick 6 could easily pay six or seven figures.

The first two Breeders' Cup races were won by the favorites paying $5.60 and $3.60. The third race started the Ultra Pick 6 and it was a one-mile race on the turf. The favorite in that race, Rock of Gibraltar, was beaten by a 26-to-1 shot called Domedriver.

Starting off the Pick 6 with a $54 mutuel eliminated most of the live tickets, making the five out of six consolations the best those gamblers could do. Three quarters of the net pool is divided between those having a ticket with all six winning horses. The remaining quarter is paid to those having tickets with five winners in the six races.

The six-furlong sprint was next and the favorite named Orientate won and paid $7.40. Another turf race followed and was won by another long shot named Starine, at a price of $28.40. This wiped out most of the Pick 6 tickets and a lot of the consolations. After the fourth leg of the Pick 6, which was won by the third choice on the board paying $10.20, a scan from the Autotote hub was sent to Arlington which showed how many Pick 6 tickets were still live up to the last two races.

The reason the Pick 6 wagers were not transmitted immediately to the host track tote system was because the large amounts of data would bog down the tote computers.

Every ticket is live before the first leg; after the fourth leg most tickets are dead (losers). Figures representing the amount of money wagered in the pool are sent right away; then, after four races are complete, a scan is sent showing only the live tickets.

Keith, Jack, and I were in the tote room when the scan came over. We were all speculating about how many bettors were still alive in the Pick 6 and the general consensus was "not too many."

After Keith looked at the scan, he said, "You won't believe this." One lucky bettor wagering at the Catskill's off-track betting parlor in upstate New York had one $12 ticket alive with all the horses in the fifth leg (eight) and all the horses in the last leg (twelve). No one else in the country had the first four winners in their Pick 6s.

We were all dumbfounded that one bettor in New York was smart enough to have the Pick 6 locked up—not one time, but six times—and everybody else in the country was out. Something was rotten in Denmark.

The stench of dead fish got even stronger when Keith informed us that the bettor had singled (bet only one horse) in each of the first four legs of the Pick 6, and then used all the horses in the last two legs. We all knew that something was wrong, but we didn't know how it was wrong.

Here was the first obvious problem with the mysterious ticket: No gambler in his right mind makes more than a $2 minimum ticket wager in a Pick 6. Even if the Pick 6 races looked to be won by all favorites, I don't believe that anyone would make a $12 wager, especially on Breeders' Cup with so many possible combinations. The cost of the ticket was $1,152 ([1x1x1x1x8x12=96] x12). A similar $2 ticket would have cost $192 (8x12x2) and left open the option to add more horses in the earlier races, spending up to the same amount of money while increasing the odds of winning.

The second problem was with the configuration of the ticket. A $12 ticket using only one horse in each of the first four legs and all the horses in the last two legs is not a logical ticket. No one is that sure for four consecutive races and then totally clueless on the last two.

After the fifth leg was run and won by the heavy favorite—High Chaparral paying $3.80—it seemed pretty obvious that the "fix was in" prior to the last race. The bettor was smart enough to single out two long shots—Domedriver at $54 and Starine at $28—but couldn't narrow down the field for the stone-cold favorite in the fifth leg.

Volponi, the longest shot of the day, won the last race and paid $89. The powers that be decided that they had to put up the prices for the Pick 6 and the consolation for five out of six on the tote board.

The Pick 6 paid $428,392 for each winning ticket and the consolation paid $4,606. This meant that the mystery man's $12 ticket was worth $2,570,352 (or $428,392 for each pick) and he also had 108 consolation tickets (5/6) totaling $497,448 (or $4,606 each). At that moment, we knew the mysterious winner had no chance in hell of getting paid.

The grand total before taxes was $3,067,821, which the winner had no idea he would never receive. I can just imagine him celebrating his $3 million score that night.

One of my jobs at Arlington included settlements with other racetracks or off-track betting parlors on the Arlington meet. Once a month, tracks and OTBs that took wagers on Arlington races would call and information was exchanged on whether Arlington was owed money from losing wagers or whether money was to be transferred out for the winning wagers bet at other locations.

First thing Monday morning I received a call from the settlement person at the Catskills OTB. They wanted to know when we would be sending the $3 million so that they could pay their lucky customer. Since the investigation was just getting started, I was pretty much under a gag order. I remember commenting that it would probably take a week.

By November 1, the stories were everywhere, from the racing form to the national news. Autotote, whose tote system was in the Catskills OTB, had fired an employee described as a "rogue engineer" that they claimed had access to the system to modify tickets. Also, the winning bettor, who was a computer technician, was the same age and had attended the same university as the Autotote employee. They were in a fraternity together. What are the odds?

The winning bettor maintained his innocence with his attorney issuing this statement: "As far as he is concerned he made a legitimate bet, the race was run and he won, he should have received his payoff and that should be the end of it. Now, instead, there's an investigation, people are making wild accusations, and his reputation is being sullied for no good reason." Is it a wonder that people distrust lawyers?

Three weeks later the not-guilty plea from the Autotote programmer was changed to guilty. A deal was struck with the New York prosecuting attorney for a greatly reduced sentence. In his guilty plea he admitted to placing other Pick 6 and Pick 4 bets and altering them after the fact. He also printed up fake tickets using the serial numbers of un-cashed tickets that had been in the system for a long time. The scheme had gone on for about a year and worked well enough for him to pay off his house and car.

Most criminals get caught because they go to the well once too often. These two had a pretty nice scam going, but wanted that really big score, and what better day than Breeders' Cup day to get it. They only got caught because they lacked gambling logic. Their plan seemed to end at producing winning tickets.

This scam could have succeeded if the plan included a better understanding of the wagering system and the bets that set up red flags. It's kind of like the IRS. If you stray too far from a known pattern, you get audited.

First of all, they opened their wagering account two days before the Breeders' Cup and only made one bet that day, on the Ultra Pick 6. That's a big red flag. They should have had the account opened for a month or so and made some "losing" Pick 6 wagers, spending more than a few dollars—that's the seed money necessary for any good scam.

Second of all, no gambler (especially one who has a wagering account) would make a $12 Pick 6 ticket when the minimum bet is only $2. They did this for one reason and one reason only: greed. A bigger red flag is having the only winning tickets not once, but six times. They probably thought that there would be other winners and instead of being one winner in five and collecting 20% of the pool, they could have six tickets out of ten and receive 60% of the pool

This should have become obvious after the first four legs of the Pick 6 produced two long shots. Right then and there they should have realized they might have the only live ticket. Whether you have a $2 ticket or a $12 ticket, you get the whole pool if you're the only winner.

Last but not least, the biggest gaffe on their part was not adding more horses in the earlier races. This could have easily been accomplished by cutting down the ticket to $2, which they should have done anyway. They spent $1,152 on their $12 straight ticket, when there was a better way to spend the same amount of money and not arouse as much suspicion.

Let's examine a theory: By using three horses in the first leg—the favorite, second or third choice, and Domedriver (the eventual winner paying $54)—it appears that you got lucky with your third pick winning. You can now single Orientate in the second leg, as he was the favorite. In the third leg, again use the favorite and throw in Starine, the actual winner. Again, it looks like you just got lucky with your second choice paying $28. In the fourth leg singling Vindication would not arise suspicion, as he was third choice paying $10.20. The last two legs are the same using all the horses.

Now let's see how much that costs: 3x1x2x1x8x12(2)=$1152, which is the same amount as the original bet. This ticket looks odd, but provides you with a much better chance of flying under the radar. After all, if questioned, you could always argue that the first four races were easier to handicap than the last two. Volponi winning the last race and paying $89 proves that point.

Being the only ticket alive after four races didn't help their cause. A few more live bettors might have made the waters murkier. They were smart enough to come up with the scam, but not smart enough to avoid the red flags by using common gamblers' logic.

The money from the Breeders' Cup Pick 6 pools was frozen by Arlington Park and put into an interest-bearing account. During an investigation, a third co-conspirator was indicted for similar scams at different racetracks.

The three pleaded guilty and the brains behind the operation, the inside man at Autotote, got the shortest sentence, one year and one day. The lucky bettor whose lawyer claimed that he was being persecuted and his reputation "sullied" got the longest sentence of thirty-seven months. There was some poetic justice.

After the sentencing, the money was available to be paid out and the seventy-eight legitimate winners holding five out of six were paid an additional $35,699 including interest. Adding the $4,606 that they were originally paid, that total of $40,305 might be the largest consolation Pick 6 ever.

25

Lenny the Schmo

In Chapter 2, I talked about the futility of betting on a horse to show, particularly long shots. There is a certain type of gambler that loves betting to show, especially favorites. Since the chalk (favorite) usually hits the board (first, second, or third) about 70% of the time, their logic is to just bet them to show and collect seven out of ten bets.

Some smart gamblers might think that they can improve on those numbers and maybe pick eight or nine out of ten to run at least third. They'd do a lot of collecting and probably wouldn't have long losing streaks. However, if an average payoff were $3 to show, then for every ten $2 bets made there'd be a profit of $1. Seven winners at $3 each equal $21 less the $20 spent on the ten races, which leaves that lonely buck.

In order to make a decent profit one would have to bet $100 to $200 each race just to make $50 to $100 on every ten bets. If that's not enough profit, the bet has to be increased to $400 to show to make $200 for those same ten bets. At this point our gambler is starting to turn into a "schmo." Roughly defined, a schmo is deficient in judgment and good sense.

When using the 70% show ratio, the break even on the wager is $2.86 (20/7=2.86). Most racetracks will round down (break) and actually pay $2.80. The larger the bet, the more the breakage takes away from any profit.

Unfortunately, there are too many show prices of $2.20 and $2.40 to drag the average under the break-even point of $2.86. In order to compensate for that, show bettors would have to pass up the favorites and try to find non-favorites to run third. Changing tactics now makes the original statistic—seven out of ten favorites hit the board—no longer valid for the new betting pattern.

The problem with this whole mindset is that there are a lot of other schmos out there trying to do the same thing. The only way anyone can justify betting this way is if they truly believe they are smarter than all the other chalk bettors.

The one wild card in this whole equation is that horseracing is unlike any other sports wager. The more you bet on a horse the less it pays (Big Louie). Betting $400, $500, and $600 to show can knock down the average mutuel from $3 to $2.80. That might be enough to take a winning strategy and turn it into a losing one. Sticking to large pools at better racetracks with the quality horses, $600 might not drop the mutuel below that breakeven Mason-Dixon line.

With that in mind, there are only two ways that a racetrack can lose money. One is to be robbed (Howie?), and the other is when a large bet on one horse creates a minus pool. Tracks guarantee a $2.10 payoff for every $2 winning bet. When there isn't enough in the mutuel pool to satisfy all the winners, the track has to make up the difference. Large wagers in the show pool can create minus pools.

In the early 1990s the original super schmo was a lawyer from New Jersey. He would fly into Chicago once or twice a year to make a large wager. The bet was $100,000 to show on some favorite. If his horse finished in the money he would collect the show price of $2.10 and get back $105,000 for his original bet of $100,000, which netted him a $5,000 profit.

The New Jersey lawyer must have thought he had found some magic formula for beating the races. But think about it: if he made nineteen straight winning show bets and if the twentieth horse ran out (off the board) he ends up losing $5,000. If number 21 runs out, it's now $105,000 in the loss column.

What if he lost two out of the first four bets? He'd be out $190,000 and would need thirty-eight straight show winners to break even. In all my years at the racetrack, this was about the dumbest bet that I had ever seen. The New Jersey lawyer fell off the radar. As a betting man, I'd say his show system went bust.

I thought I'd never see another schmo until Lenny showed up at Arlington Park. For a gambler who was betting $5,000 to $10,000 to show on chalks, one would think he could afford his own racing form instead of scavenging for one in the trash. That aside, he managed to do really well the first year and then began to increase his wagering. The racetrack saw the mutuel handle increase; thanks to Lenny's show bets totaling $40,000 to $50,000 a day.

His large wagers coincided with the newly established rebate program at Arlington, which was designed to keep big bettors wagering at the track and not with offshore betting services. Lenny would get a rebate of 1.9% on every dollar that he bet. This turned out to be a "schmo-like" move on the part of marketing.

Every month like clockwork he would receive a voucher for as much as $15,000 for the 1.9% of his monthly total. While watching the monthly handle increase with the blinkers on, nobody else took notice of the minus pools that he was creating.

With my boss's blessing I began to track Lenny's wagers like a bloodhound on the hunt. It turned out that between the minus pools and the rebate, the track was losing more than the increased handle brought in. I also tracked Lenny's bets and even with the rebate he was barely breaking even.

It turned out the track was losing, and Lenny was losing. The only winners were those betting to show on all the other horses in the races when his horse ran off the board. In those races horses were paying double-digit mutuels to show. On one occasion I added up the three show prices and they totaled over $200. The sharper bettors across the United States who could actually handicap started to get involved, and the huge show prices were going down but were still quite decent.

To stop the bleeding, the plug had to be pulled on rebating bettors when minus pools were created. Even with the facts in hand, it took the marketing department about six months to finally cancel Lenny's 1.9% rebate. Instead of doing it immediately, the track gave him one month's notice. That final month he wagered up to $200,000 a day. With his own finish line in sight, Lenny threw caution to the wind, got out his whip, and bet on any favorite to show that came close to meeting his minimum requirements. With this new betting strategy and the impending loss of the rebate, Lenny's bankroll was headed for life support.

There are too many things that can go wrong in a horse race (I personally have seen them all, some firsthand) and only a schmo would use a system that requires cashing twenty winners out of twenty-one races just to break even.

26

One Man's Trash,
Another Man's Treasure

I first met Charlie the Pool Closer around 2002 at Arlington Park. He worked next to the mutuel office in the tote room. His job was to make sure that the pools were closed after every race. Arlington Park had hired independent pool closers as a precaution on non-live racing days when they handled simulcast racing (from out-of-state racetracks) starting in 1995. The incident with Big Louie was partly the reason; the other was that there were too many tracks for the tote to watch on the non-live racing days.

Charlie sat in front of a dozen televisions and watched the simulcast races go off, and then made sure that the pools were previously closed by the system. It was a double check to ensure the integrity of the system. The job was pretty boring and he had time between races to read or do whatever.

One day Charlie came up to me with this great system to win at the dog races and he wanted to know what I thought about it. He had been charting all the results of the Trifectas at Dairyland Dog Track, located across the border in Wisconsin. It appeared to him that a lot of the Trifectas were paying big prices, sometimes in thousands of dollars.

His system was simple: he would box (bet all combinations) all the dogs in the race assuring him the winning Trifecta ticket. With eight dogs in the standard race, the cost was $336 (8x7x6). This would guarantee him a winner and the big ones would more than make up for those that paid under $336, which would drain his bankroll. The plan was perfect, no handicapping was involved; as anyone who has bet dogs knows, it's really a numbers game anyway.

Charlie gave me his handwritten list of all the Trifecta payoffs and, at first glance, it appeared to be profitable. He would need a decent bankroll to start in case the initial winners paid less than his original bet. After all, the ones that paid $100 to $200 would start costing him money when he was betting $336 a pop. As I tried to find faults in the system, both Tommy's and Sammy's gambling schemes came to mind. There had to be a hidden flaw in Charlie's logic.

After sleeping on it overnight, the light bulb went on the next day. What Charlie had failed to add into his equation was that those Trifectas he was charting would not be his payoffs because of the extra winner—Charlie himself.

In other words, if the net Trifecta pool was $2,000 and there were two winners, then each winner received $1,000 for the ticket. Adding Charlie's money to the pool would increase it by about $250 ($336 minus commissions of 25%) for a total of $2,250. Divide that by three winners and the Trifecta pays $750, not $1,000. That means that all the Trifectas in the study would be lower, with the largest ones taking the biggest hit.

Because dog racing had very small pools, it was not uncommon for only one person to have the only winning Trifecta in the race. For example, if the pool was $2,000, with one winner getting it all, adding another winner cuts that tri down to $1,125. That meant Charlie could toss the list of past Trifectas in the garbage because it was meaningless.

My logic escaped poor Charlie and I think that he tried his system anyway. About a month later I asked him how his dog racing system was working out and he didn't want to talk about it.

Charlie was the only full-time pool closer and he took the job more seriously than the part-timers. He was there Monday through Friday on time, and he never missed a day of work. Besides closing pools he was constantly cleaning up the mess from the night crew and after his shift. He would take out the trash, old programs, and printouts from the tote machine deck writer to the dumpsters on the back dock. Charlie seemed like a model employee.

That being said, one Saturday in June after the third race I was stunned to see Charlie being escorted to the mutuel office by two security guards. One of the guards was carrying a briefcase similar to the one Charlie toted to work every day. I looked at Charlie and asked, "What are you doing here on your day off?" He didn't respond as he was ushered into the manager's office. The door closed behind him. It was never a good sign when someone went into the inner sanctum and the door closed. When the window blinds went down, I knew it wasn't good for poor Charlie.

For the life of me I could not figure out what Charlie could have possibly done wrong. One thing about the racetrack is that you don't have to wait very long to find anything out. An Arizona brushfire doesn't spread as fast as a racetrack rumor. I went into the tote room to get the skinny and the boys already had the story.

Once a season, Arlington Park liked to have a mystery voucher day. What this entailed was sending out a voucher to patrons in the track's database. The mutuel department would print up the vouchers and the marketing department did the mailings. There was no amount on the voucher, but a letter with the voucher explained the day it was good for and the minimum and maximum amount that it could be worth. The minimum was $5 and I think that the max was $50.

The track usually did the mailing a month in advance of the particular day that the vouchers could be cashed. The object was to get the customers to come out on that particular day and reward them with a minimum of $5, which hopefully they would use for their first bet.

They told me that Charlie was standing in front of a self-service machine for twenty minutes running mystery vouchers through the machine. He had a briefcase full of them and the customers behind him who were trying to place a bet complained to the security guards. They in turn radioed for an Arlington manager to come up and see what was going on. Since only one mystery voucher was sent to each household, Charlie had some explaining to do.

His explanation was a simple one. While taking out the garbage one day during the previous week, he noticed hundreds of unopened envelopes in the dumpster. They were the mystery vouchers that had been mailed out a month ago, but were returned to Arlington

Park by the postal service and marked "Address Unknown," or "No Forwarding Address."

The envelopes were sealed, but on the outside they indicated that there was a mystery voucher inside. Charlie opened one up and, sure enough, there was a voucher inside and a letter stating the only day that it was redeemable—that Saturday.

Charlie scooped hundreds of envelopes from the dumpster, placed them in his briefcase, and took them home. "Finders keepers" was Charlie's defense. Who in their right mind would *not* pick up a $5 bill lying on the street or in the garbage? What is the difference between finding in the garbage five-dollar bills or vouchers worth five dollars? Charlie had stumbled into a gold mine and all he had to do was figure out how to get the gold out.

Similar to his Dairyland Dog Track Trifecta scheme, Charlie didn't put much thought into how to cash the vouchers. How would five hundred or so customers cash those vouchers on that Saturday? he should have asked himself. Some might come early to the track, some later. They might use self-service machines to cash the vouchers for either a bet or another voucher, once they discover the mystery amount. Some might go to tellers and just redeem them for cash on their first bet. One thing for sure is that they would have been cashed throughout the day and through many different machines.

Charlie didn't have a plan. He went to a self-service machine and started feeding the vouchers into the machine. Like some slot machine junkie, he was mesmerized as the totals kept adding up. Five dollars for this one, $10 for the next one, then a $25 voucher popped up.

He was on a roll and couldn't stop, oblivious to everyone around him. He never even noticed that the security guards and the Arlington Park manager had been standing behind him. After his total on the machine went over $4,000, the free ride came to an end. They cashed out Charlie and escorted him down to the mutuel office.

Poor Charlie was fired for theft, although I would not call garbage picking stealing. I felt sorry for the guy, and thought that the person or persons responsible for putting live vouchers in the trash prior to expiration should have been fired instead. After all, they wouldn't have thrown cash into the dumpster; why live vouchers?

I told my boss that I was very curious as to how those vouchers got into the trash. He just gave me that "why don't you just let it go" look, but he also knew that I was on one of my quests. I would not rest until I uncovered the entire story.

When you want to know something at Arlington you go see Vidal, who ran the loading dock and mailroom. As all mail goes in and out through him, he would know what happened. He was always the first to know who was getting let go, who was quitting, and who was being hired. He was plugged in, that's for sure.

I went to Vidal's office on the loading dock and he was in there wrapping packages. "Hey Vidal, how's it hanging?" I asked. "Hey Jimmy," he replied, "What can I do for you?" I always got along well with Vidal and we joked around a lot.

I talked about Charlie and asked Vidal point blank if he knew how the returned envelopes ended up in the trash. He responded that he threw them out. I was surprised and asked why he would toss them. The story that followed didn't surprise me, not after twenty-eight years at the racetrack.

The mystery mailer had gone out about a month ago, with Vidal handling the mass mailing. A week later he told me that the envelopes started coming back marked "no name at that address," and "unknown"; and all were stamped "return to sender." He took them back to the marketing department every day and put them on the desk of "the person in charge."

This went on for weeks and they were piling up. Finally, the Wednesday before the mystery voucher day, Vidal was told to not bring any more in and to throw the lot out. Vidal didn't question the contents of the envelopes and did what he was told.

After the fact, the marketing department "circled the wagons" and no one was fired. As far as I knew, no one even got a slap on the wrist. For weeks, as the story circulated, people speculated as to what they would have done had they found the vouchers. Everyone had a little larceny in his or her heart, but no one admitted outright that they would have cashed the vouchers. The one thing that everyone agreed upon was a plan with better execution. And it was mentioned that the marketing department could use a shredder.

27

The Elusive Pick 6

When the first Pick 6 wager was introduced in 1983 at Hollywood Park, it was called the Perfect 6. For a mere $2, and picking six winners in a row, bettors could win thousands of dollars, similar to a lotto ticket. Some Pick 6 payouts have been more than $1 million—not bad for two bucks!

Two drawbacks to the wager are the number of consecutive races that one has to pick winners in (six) and the original amount of the bet ($2). The Pick 6 usually encompasses the last six races on the card, which normally include a feature race. This race is always the most competitive and generally has full fields. The bigger the fields, the harder the Pick 6 is to hit. Also, the last race on the card is commonly a maiden race (of horses who have never won), which is harder to handicap. In many of those races there are first time starters that have no running lines to study.

As I shared in the "Summer of Saratoga" chapter, the cost of betting two horses in every race is $128. Some might feel confident having covered two horses in each race.

Now let's look at the actual probability of winning a Pick 6 by calculating the total number of horses in each race. For the sake of argument, I will assume that the Pick 6 races had the following number of horses in each:

- First leg—8 horses
- Second leg—10 horses

- Third leg—7 horses
- Fourth leg—6 horses
- Fifth leg—9 horses
- Last leg—10 horses

The actually probability is 8 x 10 x 7 x 6 x 9 x 10 = 302,400 combinations. The amount it would take to buy out this particular field (bet every horse in every race) would be $604,800, assuring you one winning ticket.

A fool's bet to be sure! Unless the rest of the patrons at the track bet significant amounts of money into the pool, there probably wouldn't be enough left to cover the initial investment after the track's takeout (minimum 25% on Pick 6's). This also assumes that there is only one winner. Add another winning ticket and the prize money is reduced by half. If there were four winners, then the payout would be one quarter of the net pool.

Let's see what happens if a good handicapper could eliminate from winning about half the horses in each race. The equation then becomes 4 x 5 x 3 x 3 x 4 x 5 = 3,600 combinations x $2 for the bet, or a cost of $7,200; still too rich for the experienced horseplayer.

The average horseplayer puts between $16 and $64 into each Pick 6 wager, and usually three of the six horses selected are favorites. Using several favorites in a Pick 6 often results in a lesser payout. Even though the pool that determines the odds and the Pick 6 pools are separate, the betting public frequently mimics their wagering habits from the standard bets right through to the gimmick wagers.

With a total 302,400 possible winning combinations in the above example, the odds of the $128 (sixty-four combinations) bet is still 4,725 to 1 to win. Doesn't seem like a good bet now, does it? A professional handicapper can cut down on those fields and eliminate more than half of the horses that they feel have no chance to win. This can sometimes backfire when one of those un-winnable horses ends up crossing the wire first. That Pick 6 can then be quite large and sometimes the whole pool goes to one lucky patron (often not the professional).

I came close to winning the Pick 6 two times after that fated day at Saratoga. The first was at Santa Anita Park in Arcadia, California, in 2003 when the track was guaranteeing a $1 million Pick 6 pool.

My friend Tony was going to take a stab at it one day and called and asked if I wanted a piece of his $1,920 ticket. I told him I'd put up $192 and take 10% of the action (whatever it paid). Spending $1,920 gave us plenty of combinations ([5 x 4 x 4 x 3 x 2 x 2 = 960] x $2 = $1,920). Tony had hit a few Pick 6s in the past, but he had to spend some money to get them.

We had the first five winners by surviving a photo finish in the fourth leg. I'm normally at the wrong end of the horse when it comes to photos, so I thought Tony just might be my good luck charm. Santa Anita, like most racetracks, paid a consolation on 5/6 winners, so we were guaranteed to collect something. In the last race we had two horses going, the lone speed horse and a closer. Our two Pick 6 probable payoffs were around $30,000 and $28,000, my end being 10% of that.

Before the race I called Tony and asked him if there was any horse that worried him and that we should play to protect our investment. Since the last race was a maiden race (non-winners) and a big field with twelve horses, we decided to sit tight and hope for the best.

The last race was a six-furlong race (sprint race) and turning for home our lone speed horse was in front by four lengths. The only two horses that had a chance to catch him were our other selection and a first-time starter. Halfway to the wire our lead horse started to shorten stride; he was getting tired. The first-time starter was running green in the stretch (running erratically) and our other horse had flattened out (quit).

Somehow Jon Court, the jockey on the first-time starter, got his horse straightened out and he nipped us in a photo finish. He was 25 to 1 and the Pick 6 paid more than $100,000. Having two live horses in the last race we received the 5 out of 6 payoff twice. At $900 a ticket, we got back $1,800, losing $120 on the total cost of the ticket. I ended up losing only $12, but that was no consolation.

A couple of years later I was playing Hollywood Park in California and they also guaranteed a $1 million Pick 6 pool. I took a shot myself at the Pick 6 because the races looked very beatable. I was only going to spend a little bit so I bet a $64 ticket ([2 x 2 x 2 x 1 x 2 x 2 = 32] x $2).

My only single was in the fourth leg and it was a grass race. The horse was a long shot at 10 to 1, but he really looked good. The horses I picked in the other races were first, second, or third betting choices, so I didn't expect the Pick 6 to pay a lot. But, if my long shot won in the twelve-horse grass race, the payoff could be decent.

I got the first three winners in easily, but no mutuel payout was more than $9. The important race for me was coming up. My horse was going off at 14 to 1 running out of the number 3 post and the favorite was at 9/5 running out of post position 12.

The two things that I knew about Hollywood Park's turf course at the time were that horses with the lead in the stretch usually held on, and the outside post positions had a terrible winning percentage.

The speed held up because the turf was firm and hard, and the outside was not good because the horses usually got a bad trip from there. Either they were forced wide on the first turn or they had to drop back out of the gate and had too much ground to make up in the stretch.

My horse had the perfect trip in the race—he broke third and stayed on the rail, then coming for home drew out in the stretch. The favorite had a horrible trip in the race. Out of the gate he dropped back to last, was last on the backside, and when they turned for home was forced 9 wide with 6 lengths to make up in a short Hollywood Park stretch.

By now you must have figured out who won the race—the favorite by a head. I watched the replay three times and still couldn't figure out how that horse got up to win. He had the worst trip and my horse had the perfect trip, but somehow I got beat.

Now my only salvation was to hope that my last two picks would lose. I knew that if they both won I'd get paid for having picked 5/6, but it wouldn't pay much. That would also mean I lost a decent-paying Pick 6 by a head.

It's funny how when I want a horse to lose, I just seem to know that he's going to win. I sat and watched as my two picks in the eighth race ran first and second and ditto for the ninth race. The Pick 6 containing mostly favorites paid $1,200. If my $30 horse had won the seventh race, the Pick 6 could have paid more than $5,000. I cashed the consolation ticket twice, collecting a whopping $78. Chump change.

My wife, who has yet to acknowledge the appeal of horseracing, has a different take on the Pick 6. She argues that if I can't pick three or four winners in a day, what are the chances of picking six in a row? I know there's probably real logic in her thinking based on my past history, but the siren song of that gimmick bet is sometimes just too hard to resist.

28

Win, Place, or Show

Throughout my life I was never much of a favorite player and usually tried to beat the horse with the lowest odds on the board with a better-priced horse. If the favorite was going off at 2 to 1, I would look for a logical horse with odds between 4 to 1 and 8 to 1. I'm sure that I subliminally picked this up from my father and Uncle Dick, who were not "chalk rats." After I retired, I began a project investigating whether betting favorites could actually have a positive outcome.

One of the handicapping services stated that its calculated numbers—which combined speed, class, pace, form, distance and a myriad of other handicapping factors into one easy number—had very favorable results. The claim of a 55% win ratio for any horse having a 10 plus point advantage over the next closest horse in the same race got my attention. In layman's terms, this meant that the two highest handicapped numbers would have to be 10 points apart (for example, 126 and 116). If there was a 6 plus point advantage, the win ratio was 46%. Even a 3 plus point advantage still yielded a healthy 39% win ratio.

The service claimed that their numbers were tested over tens of thousands of races. Their only caveat was that only dirt racing, not Turf racing, was used in their study. What they neglected to divulge was whether or not their return on investment, or ROI, was positive. In other words, could you make a profit betting on those horses that had a 3, 6, or 10-point advantage over their next rated pick? This was something that inquiring minds wanted to know. Well, at any rate, I did!

With plenty of free time on my hands, it was time to kill two birds with one stone. I could test the service's claim *and* find out if the chalk player knew something that I didn't know about the wisdom of betting favorites. My quest was to find races with those point differentials between two horses and track the outcomes. Would too much information be a good thing?

I assumed that most of the horses with big number advantages would be either favorites or second choices, based on the service's handicapping method. I wasn't expecting any bombers (long shots) in the mix.

I started my project by spending seven days a week for three months tracking the numbers. Twenty racetracks in all were used and all races were dirt only. The only factor that I changed was that I omitted maiden races. These races have many first-time starters and very little information on horses that ran once or twice. I was hoping to improve on the handicapping service's percentage by avoiding the maiden races.

After studying 854 bets across that time span, my results showed:

Jim	3 plus = 37% winners (excluding maiden races)
Service	3 plus = 39% winners (all races)
Jim	6 plus = 49% winners (excluding maiden races)
Service	6 plus = 46% winners (all races)
Jim	10 plus = 67% winners (excluding maiden races)
Service	10 plus = 55% winners (all races)

By tossing out the maiden races, I scored slightly lower on the 3 plus, but higher on the 6 and 10 plus differentials. All in all, their claim to giving a good percentage of winners was absolutely true. The big question remained: Would you make any money with all those winners?

Here are the cold hard facts: I showed 360 winners, 542 horses tracked ran first or second and 621 hit the board (ran first, second or third). Those percentages overall were 42% win, 63% place, and 73% show. The average mutuel payout was $4.35 win, $2.90 place, and $2.36 show. Based on a $2 wager, the losses were $142 on win bets, $136 on place bets, and $242 on the show end.

What did I learn from all this analysis? I could cash more win bets in three months (360) than I probably did in the last thirty years, and still not show a profit. As I've previously pointed out, betting to show was the worst bet of them all. I only needed to listen to my elders.

The prudent course of action would have been to do the study and digest the results. Prudence has never been one of my finer qualities. I started making a few wagers along the way during my research. I have never been a strict $2 bettor, so starting there I quickly advanced to $5, then $10, only to end up back at $2. Early on the numbers were better than later. I did have a budget, which also determined the wagered amounts during a slow spell. Like my Aunt Florence, I have a tendency to take the bull by the horns. Why wait when I can jump in on the action now? The following story explains.

The first time my family went to Las Vegas in a group, Aunt Florence was in her seventies and had never flown on an airplane. She and Uncle Dick had been to Las Vegas many years before but had taken the train, since she was afraid to fly. There were twenty of us going for Thanksgiving, to celebrate turkey day in Sin City, and we weren't taking the train. She relented and got on the airplane with the group and was pleasantly surprised by how quickly she could be gambling, only four hours after leaving Chicago.

One night I was playing blackjack with Flo and the only open tables required a $25 minimum bet. We sat down, the dealer gave her $200 in green ($25) chips, and she started betting $50 and $75 a hand. I reminded her that the she could make a minimum bet of $25. She looked at me and replied, "I can't bet just one chip." So you see, it's simple: I couldn't bet just $2. It's not in the genes.

29

You Can Beat a Race, Not the Races

TVG is an interactive horseracing network that combines live televised coverage from more than sixty of America's premier racetracks. It has brought the convenience of wagering to the relaxed atmosphere of home by phone, the Web, and (where available) set-top remote control. It debuted in September 1999 and it is currently available in twelve states. California is its home base and probably has the biggest fan base.

TVG is available to watch through Dish Network, Direct TV, and select cable systems. Arlington Park Race Track carried it on its satellite like any other racetrack feed. Since racetracks have the ability to go directly to other contracted racetracks and show that track's own announcers and handicappers, customers rarely requested TVG feed.

While flipping through the channels at work, I would see the station, but never kept it on. TVG was not available for wagering in Illinois, so I had no interest in it. I figured that if I wanted to be touted, why not go directly to the Churchill Downs channel and absorb all the "inside" racing opinions from its "experts."

After retiring and moving to Arizona in late 2005, I didn't have the convenience of having all the tracks on my TV as I did when I worked at the track, or the availability of making that occasional wager. Other services provided legal Internet wagering similar to TVG. However, my new DSL service had problems receiving streaming video.

Under most circumstances, betting a race without watching it seemed rather pointless to me. Imagine betting on a football game or any other sporting event and then turning on a movie instead of watching your wager in action. Unless there's a funeral (and it better be somebody close) that just isn't going to happen. I had to find a way to see the races that I wanted to bet on, and Direct TV solved my problem.

For a mere $10 a month I could subscribe to a sports channel that offered TVG in its package. Most, but not all, of the races I might consider betting would now be shown on my home television. For $120 a year, it seemed like a good deal. By January 1 I was up and running. Gulfstream Park in Florida was opening on January 3 and I was ready. Unfortunately, TVG was not.

Having handicapped the opening day card, I was quite surprised when I turned on TVG to watch the first race, and Gulfstream Park was nowhere to be found. I went to the TVG website and it wasn't on their programming guide. It seemed that they had no contract with Gulfstream Park and were not allowed to show the races.

I called Bob, the TVG guru, and he told me that they didn't carry the winter meet at Santa Anita either. No contract, even though they carried the fall Oak Tree meet at that same track.

How could they carry one meet at a racetrack and not another? Two key racetracks running in the winter and as a TVG subscriber or viewer, I could not watch these races. Ten dollars a month wasn't looking like much of a deal after all. The one silver lining was that since the tracks I wanted to bet (Gulfstream, Santa Anita), weren't carried by TVG, I wasn't being touted by their *experts*.

During that time I stuck mostly to turf racing at both tracks and bet only two or three races a day. I found "Race Replays," a free service where I was able to watch the replays of the races. I reasoned that after-the-fact viewing was better than nothing. By the end of April I showed a profit of about $700 for the first four months. At that time I didn't realize how lucky I was.

With May came the opening of Churchill Downs and all the TVG tracks were in full swing. At 9:00 a.m. Arizona time, the TVG show from the east coast began. The announcers were paired in twos and as soon as the first race was available for wagering, out came the expert opinions. With races going off every ten minutes, announcers' picks came fast and furious, and they all made perfect sense. They read the form and dissected it for the viewer. They showed prior races and explained why the certain horses were ready to win. Trainers were also interviewed to give that extra insight.

The on-air announcers were made up of ex-jockeys, trainers, old handicappers, pretty women, racetrack announcers, you name it. They had someone for everyone. They had their share of winners, but like an old cashier I once knew said, "If you throw enough shit on the fan, something's gotta stick." Like monkeys in a cage they were flinging it fast and furious all day long.

At noon Arizona time, TVG had a special show where one particular announcer handicapped something like twelve races in an hour. Every five minutes a race would go off; win or lose that announcer was just as enthusiastic about the next horse, waving his arms and running around on the set. When the hour was up he was physically spent, his mood swings from winning to losing taking a toll.

Some days his picks were right on, but most days the dartboard method would have given him a run for his money. Another particular sage gave out two horses a day, and if subscribers didn't show a profit betting those picks to win and place, they would receive the difference back in their TVG wagering account. I don't recall that guarantee lasting very long.

Eight hours later, around 5:00 p.m., after the last race went off at Hollywood Park on the west coast, TVG had aired between seventy-five and eighty races, from eight or ten different racetracks around the country, and gave nonstop expert opinions on every single race. I—along with many other viewers—became what I termed "TVG numb."

The biggest promotion at the time was the Pick 4. Twice a day TVG had two guaranteed Pick 4s at two separate racetracks, usually the best tracks of the day. At this time it was Churchill Downs and Hollywood Park. They would guarantee the pools of the second Pick 4 at each track to be about $250,000. This was a great promotion for them and would encourage the bettors to wager these gimmicks, knowing that pool would have a specified amount in it. If the mutuel pool was not large enough, TVG made up the difference.

Each on-air handicapper was encouraged to put together a mythical Pick 4 ticket for the viewers. They weren't allowed to go over $50 for the total cost of the ticket, which was made available both online and on the air. This went on all day, and not just for the guaranteed races. By day's end, a bettor could have invested between $600 and $800 if he actually followed the sages' picks.

The experts had their share of winners. When they happened to be large-priced ones, viewers certainly heard about it on the broadcast for weeks. The astute handicapper was repeatedly congratulated.

In the past, TVG posted the results of the experts' mythical Pick 4s on its website. This showed each handicapper's name; with a running total of how much they were ahead or behind based on actual race results. Since they all eventually went into the red (showing losses) that practice was wisely discontinued.

I believe that using picks from a "personality" with a big following really has no value; the bigger the expert, the better the reason not to make that wager. What I mean is that when a particular handicapper does have a Pick 4 winner with his on-air ticket, it will generally pay less than one he didn't give out. The fact that the experts don't show a profit in the long run proves this point. I know this may sound confusing, but follow my logic.

Let's assume that there is $200,000 in the Pick 4 mutuel pool after the track's takeout. Let's also assume that there are forty winning tickets without the expert's selection. The Pick 4 pays $5,000 per ticket ($200,000 divided by 40). If the winning numbers coincide with the expert's selection and forty of his followers nationwide played his choice, then there would be eighty winning tickets. That reduces the payoff to $2,500, or half of what it would have paid had the expert not had the winner.

Following the TV personalities isn't necessarily "baaaaaad," but it often creates that sheep-herd mentality. If the sheep decide to turn on the wolves, and refuse to be herded, then this is a useless argument. But, in my experience, there are always new sheep just waiting to be sheared.

Many gamblers swear that they would never follow the herd, but they often get hooked on all the commentary, the insiders' insight, the trainers' experience, and the constant flow of racing information. It's too much information for anyone to assimilate and use to make logical choices, but once they start, can they stop? Everyone wants that edge, that clue that will help pick a winner.

The bottom line on TVG is this: It can be very addicting. I couldn't stop watching, always getting drawn back for just one more race. If gamblers wagered on all those tips they *could* end up going broke. So instead, I cherry picked the horses that TVG recommended and which also made sense to me.

Unfortunately, that didn't work. In fact, nothing worked for me. I was throwing money at the horses and caution to the wind. It seemed like the only TVG picks that won were the horses I didn't bet on. I had officially entered horseplayers' hell and didn't realize it. I tried breaking the "habit" by not watching TVG, but before the day was up I always turned it on. I tried leaving the sound on mute, but as the voices in my head got louder I had to turn it back up.

On April 30, 2006, I was ahead $700 for the year, then came the steady diet of TVG. On July 13, after barely two and a half months of TVG, my account balance was $1.37. My January 1 starting bankroll had been wiped out plus my profit. The next day I copied the famous statement by the great Panamanian boxer Roberto Duran: "No Mas." No more. It was time to take a break from the horses (that's when I started to write the book).

I had started the year handicapping with my Uncle Dick's credo in mind: "You can beat a race, but you can't beat the races." Who would know this better than a bookmaker of thirty years? Unfortunately, with the assistance of TVG, I tried to beat *all* the races. It was an accident waiting to happen. As accidents go, I guess it could have been much worse. I came out alive and hopefully wiser. Time will only tell.

30

Bob and Jim's Wild Ride

Bob and I have known each other for more than forty years. We grew up one block apart in Elmwood Park. Three years my junior and the same age as my brother Jerry, we shared an interest (some would say an obsession) in playing cards and golf. We've managed to forge a lasting friendship. Since Bob was a harness horseplayer, a sport I gave up on years ago, we rarely gambled on horses together.

Around 2000 Bob became more involved with thoroughbreds and betting on Breeders' Cups and Derby Days. We have entered some handicapping contests together over the last couple of years and came close, but could never pull out a win.

After a couple months' break from the horses, I was pretty sure that I had the TVG monkey off my back. Football season had just started and Bob and I decided to give that survival pool one more attempt (see Chapter 22). I sent in our money and Bob was going to send me a check for his half. The check never arrived, but in its place a new horseracing plan was conceived.

We always began each new venture together with a sound plan. Sound, meaning that we actually thought it would work. We were men with plans and this time was no different. This new and improved plan had Bob taking the money he owed me, adding some to it, and putting it into one of the wagering accounts we had used together in the past. We would then both have access to the account to place bets.

We started on Friday, October 6, 2006, betting on Keeneland Racetrack's opening day of the fall meet. The foundation of the plan depended on Bob having success on opening day with me picking up the slack after that. Bob's past performance on opening days at different tracks around the country had shown remarkable winning records. His magic usually disappeared after the start of a meet, turning him into just another horseplayer who was often beat at the wire.

Starting with $150 in the account, our goal was to run it up to $600 by Breeders' Cup Day in November. Bob was already planning a weeklong trip to Arizona around the Breeders' Cup to play golf and horses, so it would be beneficial to have the money in the account just waiting for our handicapping genius.

Like Joe Namath guaranteeing a victory over the Colts in Super Bowl III, Bob delivered in spades on the first Friday in October. Hitting a Trifecta and the first Pick 4 at Keeneland, our account exceeded $850 by lunchtime. I was just a spectator as Bob was weaving his magic. Next was Santa Anita and another Trifecta, which put us over $1,000. A couple of losses later, we were under $900 and I thought we were through for the day.

I was wrong. The phone rang at 10 p.m. and Bob told me to check the account. Bob, it appeared, had not been through for the day. He hit the Pick 4 at Los Alamitos, a quarter-horse track in Los Angeles. That one paid $693, skyrocketing our account balance to $1,496—a tenfold increase in a single day. Bob was the man and the plan was working.

The next day it was my turn to jump into the fray and do some heavy lifting. Riding Bob's rush from the day before I increased the account balance to $1,840. We then took a couple of days off to bask in our good fortune. It was now time to expand our horizons.

While the original plan called for an account balance of $600 available on Breeders' Cup Day (November 4), we felt pretty good having a balance of $1,117 left in our account, although we were down one-third from the high point. When Bob arrived a couple of days before the big day, we played a few rounds of golf and handicapped the Cup. My Uncle Dick was fond of saying "study long, study wrong," but that was exactly what we did.

We studied so much that on Breeder's Cup Day we made 147 bets, and up until the last race we had cashed in on only six, which did not amount to much money. Going into the last two races, our account had dwindled to $465. We were leaking oil like an old Chevy.

There were still two Breeders' Cup races left to get even, or get stuck even worse. The one horse that we both thought stood out in all of the races that day was Invasor. He was running in the Classic, which was the last big race of the day. In that same race was a horse named Bernardini, the even-money favorite.

We decided to make two $10 Daily Doubles using two long shots in the ninth race with the horse we talked about all day, Invasor, in the last race. One of our two long shots won the ninth and the one horse we both loved, Invasor, won the last race beating the favorite Bernardini. Our $10 Daily Double returned $959, giving us a small profit for the day.

As bettors often relive their action with the ever-popular "woulda, shoulda, and coulda" scenarios, we determined the following:

- Betting $100 to win and $100 to place on the one horse we be both agreed was the best bet of the day (Invasor) would have netted us an $860 profit.
- All that time and effort spent on the other 145 bets made instead could have been invested in another round of golf. But what fun would that have been?

Over the next two weeks we managed to run the account back up to $1,833. We were living large and had dreams of grandeur. Six weeks into our run we figured that we had finally gotten a handle on the racing game. We naturally concluded that hitting a big Pick 4 was right around the corner.

In mid-November, with Bob back home in Wisconsin and me nestled in Arizona, we played the late Pick 4 at Hollywood Park in California. Investing only $20 we wagered a single horse in the first leg, four horses in the second leg, another single in the third, and five horses in the fourth and final leg. We needed our key horses to win the first and third legs; the extra picks in the second and fourth gave us some wiggle room.

Our lone pick won the first leg and we managed to squeeze out a long shot in the second leg. If our key horse (number 2) won the third leg we would have five horses in the last leg and some decent Pick 4 prices.

Our number 2 horse in the third leg led every step of the way, only to get caught in a photo finish at the wire by the number 1 horse, which was the co-favorite with our pick. What seemed like a five-minute photo did not go our way. I was playing Scrabble with my wife, her sister, and brother-in law at the time and had the TV on in the background. I jumped out of my chair screaming "wire, wire, give me the wire!" and they all looked at me like I was nuts (this happens a lot).

Our Scrabble game ended, but I asked that we wait to go to dinner until the last leg of the Pick 4 was run. Of course I had the unnatural desire to see the outcome of the final race for which I would secretly cheer against our five choices. I would hate losing the Pick 4's with our only loser being beat in a photo.

They posted the probable Pick 4 payoffs on the screen prior to the race and the ones with our picks were all good prices. One in particular that caught my eye was paying over $8,000 for the winning combination. This meant that our number 12 pick had to win the race. All I kept thinking was that I didn't want the number 12 horse to win. I really didn't want any of our horses to win, but especially not the number 12. At post time, that horse was a 50 to 1 shot, so I figured he wasn't a threat.

Unfortunately, the horseracing gods had other plans for Bob and me. We had climbed to the top of the racing mountain and now they decided to throw us off the other side. The number 12 horse won the last race and, in the process, hastened our descent down that mountain like a bobsled gaining speed and out of control. That prior race photo finish had cost us approximately eight grand.

The Scrabble entourage left for dinner at a restaurant ten minutes away. I dropped everyone off at the door and went to park the car. My cell phone rang and it was Bob, talking in a whisper. We rehashed the losing photo finish and then Bob blurted out, "Jim, it gets worse."

"How can it get any worse than losing eight grand?" I asked.

Bob went on to explain that in the last race he had bet $3 on a Superfecta (which requires picking the first four finishers in that race). After losing the photo in the Pick 4, Bob put the number 12 horse on top in a ten-cent Superfecta that paid 1/10 of the normal $1 ticket. Bob liked dime Supers because he could pick a lot of horses for a little money and still be able to get a decent payoff.

We obviously didn't cash in on the Super either, but I had to ask what it paid. The $1 Super paid $35,000, which meant that the dime wager was worth $3,500. Even with my head spinning the math was easy to do.

Another quick calculation proved that by betting on all the horses in the fourth position with his picks in the other three spots (which all won) it would have cost only another $4.20 (total cost of $7.20). Once again, saving less than a fin had cost us thousands. I hung up the phone with visions of Pick 4s and Superfectas dancing in my head, then walked into the restaurant and pretended to be hungry.

The death spiral had started and from that day on nothing went right. Every Pick 4 we played, we had three out of four; every Trifecta, two out of three. Win bets ran second and place bets ran third. By December 8, our account went below $300 and we were totally disgusted. We played very little through the rest of the month. Our balance was $268 at the end of 2006, a mere $118 profit from where we started.

All through this wild ride, I had used TVG only for the purpose of watching the races, never for the "expert" commentary. That might explain how we made that $150 last so long. On December 31, I pulled the plug on TVG by canceling my sports package. That would put me in front $10 a month, enough for a couple of winning Daily Doubles. Maybe.

31

Close, but No Cigar

In sports betting there are basically two ways to go: You can either bet individual games or bet in the future pools. To my way of thinking, betting individual games and trying to grind out a profit is best left to the professional gamblers.

In football, most bettors wager the point spread on the games. The points determine whether you're a winner, not just the team. If the New England Patriots win the game by 19 points easily, but the spread was 20, you lost your bet on New England. A tie is no bet, but football eliminates a lot of ties by throwing a "hook" on the game (for example, making the spread 7.5 points instead of 7). The half point is known as the hook; sometimes it helps you, but most of the time it hangs you.

In baseball, if you bet individual games you have to lay as much as 3 to 1 odds according to who's pitching that day. For instance, if Randy Johnson in his prime were facing a no-name pitcher from the Kansas City Royals, you might have to lay $3 to make a $1 profit. Not a good bet if you're right three times and wrong once. You'd be back to square one.

Basketball is similar to football in that you lay hoops and if your team is favored by 9, they better win by 10 for you to collect. You don't see too many hooks in basketball.

In golf, there are several ways to bet. One is a straight future bet on a particular player entered in a tournament. Another is to buy a share on a player, which trades back-and-forth as the match progresses. Opening shares can range from $1 on the unknowns and up to $25 on players such as Tiger Woods. When the tournament is over, the winners' shares are paid out at $100; all other golfers' shares are worthless. Selling or buying your shares during play can be dicey since the bid and ask spread can be large. A good example would be Tiger leading a tournament after two days: His shares might have gone from an opening price of $20 to $60, a nice profit to sell at. The catch is the bettor wanting to buy Tiger at that point might have to pay $65 a share. That's a big spread and that's where the money is made.

The following are some of my "close but no cigar" experiences in the arena of sports betting.

Golf

The best golfer on the planet right now is Tiger Woods. The question is: Could I make money betting on him? In almost all tournaments, from a betting standpoint, he is the favorite or one of the favorites. In 2006, I thought that maybe there was a way to make a profit betting on Tiger, even at short odds (which I tend to shy away from). If Tiger got hot and strung together a couple of wins in a row, I could parlay those short odds into some positive cash flow.

Right out of the box that year, Tiger won the Buick Invitational. He wasn't much of a price since he played well at that tournament in the past, winning three of the last eight. Next was the Nissan Open, but he withdrew from that tournament. In the match play that followed, he tied for ninth, but match play was never his strong suit since turning pro. It doesn't allow for players to recover from a bad round; instead they're eliminated.

For the Ford Championship at Doral Golf Course in South Florida, I bought one share of Tiger at $20 before the tournament began. Collecting my $100 after he won, I then bought two shares at $25 each for his next tournament, the Bay Hill Invitational. He didn't play very well and finished in twentieth place. I took a pass on the next two tournaments, where he tied respectively for twenty-second place and third place.

Then Tiger took some time off to be with his terminally ill father, Earl. His dad passed away on May 3, 2006. Tiger announced that his next tournament would be the U.S. Open (a major championship) on June 18. That would give him six weeks off.

Some thoroughbreds run well after a layoff and Tiger was definitely *the* thoroughbred of the golf world, so I knew that he would be ready for the U.S. Open. The odds makers seemed generous and I bought two shares at $15 each for a total of $30. I thought I was stealing something at that price! It turns out that I couldn't have been more wrong: Tiger missed the cut—only his third missed cut since 1996.

Tiger took another three weeks off and played in the Western Open at Cog Hill in suburban Chicago. This was another one of his favorite golf courses, where he had won three out of eight tournaments. (I actually attended his first victory there in 1997 and the mob of spectators following him up to the eighteenth green created quite a scene.)

I started the parlay all over again and bought two shares at $20 each. I was confident that he would rebound at the Western Open. At some point on the last day of that tournament, he had the lead but finished in a tie for second. This was an anomaly since Tiger rarely lost when in the lead on the last day.

Now I was out $40 total for my experiment and decided to pass up betting on him in the British Open. Well, Tiger Woods won the British Open *and* the next six PGA tournaments—an amazing seven straight victories. This was accomplished without my help, or maybe because of it, since I had stopped betting on him.

Tiger's streak ended after the Buick Invitational in January 2007. In between he played on a Ryder Cup team and won the Target World Challenge (a non-PGA event). Buying one share of Tiger on the British Open at $25 per share (average starting price) and having the stamina to parlay half of the winnings on the next seven PGA tournaments could have netted a gutsy gambler about $10,000 when the run was over.

Bottom line: If I had known when to start and stop, there was some money to be made on that phenomenal run, which might never happen again.

Kentucky Derby Future Pool

The Derby future pool is a tempting bet but one that is very hard to cash in on. Beginning in February, the first of three future pools are available to wager on for the Kentucky Derby, which is run the first Saturday in May. Two more pools follow in each of the next two months. Each pool may have different horses listed with the odds possibly changing on the same horse, depending upon their progress up to that point.

There may be thirty to forty horses available for wagering, but only a maximum of twenty can be entered on Derby Day. Your selection may never be entered and there is no refund. A few years ago while indulging in the future pool, I bet eight different horses at long odds, ranging from 35-1 to 75-1, spending $80. When all eight of my future picks were entered in the total field of eighteen on Derby Day, I was ecstatic. With 40% of the field covered I felt pretty confident. I stood to collect anywhere from $350 to $750 on my initial investment. After the most exciting two minutes in horseracing was over, not only did I *not* win, none of my nags even managed to hit the board!

That's why they call it gambling!

Football

The year 2007 started with the Bears playing in the Super Bowl against the Indianapolis Colts. I was holding a bet on the Bears with the odds at 25 to 1. Why, you might ask, after the 1985 Super Bowl (see Chapter 12) would I have anything to do with the Chicago Bears? The answer is that after twenty-two years, I decided to give them another chance. After all, no winning field goals were required; all they had to do was win.

My brother Jerry and Bob were high on the team that year and I was out to prove that a Green Bay Packer fan could collect a bet on their nemesis—the Chicago Bears. Also, secretly I considered it a win-win situation. If the Bears didn't win the Super Bowl, I was out half a chop ($50), which is not the end of the world. But what if the Bears did win it all? Well then, Jim the Packer fan would be collecting $1,250—a lot more than the average Bear (fan).

The Bears didn't disappoint during the fall of 2006, winning their first seven games. They went on to finish 13 and 3, losing a meaningless last game of the season to my beloved Green Bay Packers. They had a first-round bye and home-field advantage throughout the playoffs. They squeaked by the Seattle Seahawks 27 to 24 and then trounced the New Orleans Saints 39 to 14 to advance to the Super Bowl against the Indianapolis Colts.

Now it was time to hedge my bet by wagering $500 to $600 on the Colts and catch a win either way. I expected the wagering line to have the Colts as a slight favorite. Maybe the odds makers would make the Bears the favorite. No such luck. When the line came out the Colts were 7 ½ point favorites. Now I was stuck. I couldn't bet the Colts and lay 7 ½ points because if they won and didn't cover the spread I would lose *both* bets. It was the Bears or nothing.

The Super Bowl started out with a bang for the Bears when their lightening-fast return man and rookie, Devin Hester, made NFL history by returning the opening kickoff for a touchdown. But by halftime, the score was 16 to 14 with the Bears down two points. In the fourth quarter, the Colts were clinging to a 22 to 17 lead. Late in the game, the Bears marched into Colts territory and were on the verge of snatching a victory until quarterback Rex Grossman launched a horrible pass that was intercepted and returned for a Colts touchdown. Game over. The final score was 29 to 17 with the Colts, of course, covering the spread on their final touchdown. I was only out $50, but it was a bad way to start off the year.

Basketball

The Chicago Bulls became cellar dwellers once owner Jerry Reinsdorf and general manager Jerry Krause broke up the dynasty in 1998. Their vision to start from scratch with a new coach and new players caused the team to finish in last place five out of the next six years. One of the advantages of the Bulls being stinky was the high draft choice the team received as a result of last-place finishes. Those choices were beginning to pay off and by 2004 the Bulls had some good young players, such as Ben Gordon, Luol Deng, and Kurt Heinrich.

Before the 2006-2007 season began, the Bulls signed Ben Wallace, a Defensive Player of the Year four out of five years on the Detroit Pistons. Wallace was one of two missing pieces needed for the team to make a serious run for the playoffs and maybe win it all. The other piece was an inside scorer and the club was trying to trade for Kevin Garnett, the star player of the Minnesota Timberwolves.

I figured that if I waited for them to get Garnett, the odds would drop dramatically. I had to get down now while the price was right. Getting 10 to 1 on the Eastern Conference championship and 20 to 1 on the NBA championship looked pretty good to me. Betting $100 on each, I was looking at collecting $3,000 if the Bulls went all the way.

The Bulls never did land Garnett in a trade, but still went 49-33 during the 2006-2007 season and had the third best record in the Eastern conference. Being the third seed allowed the Bulls to play the first series at home against the defending NBA champions, the Miami Heat. The Bulls swept Miami, winning their first playoff series since the Michael Jordan era in the 1990s.

The next series started on the road against the Detroit Pistons (the 2004-2005 NBA champions). The Bulls mustered only one home win and lost the series four games to one. Playing more games at home in basketball, as in all sports, is a huge advantage. The Bulls needed only four more wins during the regular season to tie the Pistons at 53 and secure home-field advantage throughout the playoffs (they won the tiebreaker).

The reason that I bring this up is that the Bulls lost at least six games in which they had a big lead at halftime during the 2006-2007 season. In one of those games in particular, they had an 18-point lead against the New York Knicks. In the first five minutes of the second half, the Bulls were whistled for an unbelievable eight fouls. That helped the Knicks get back in the game, which they eventually won.

That was one of the games that Tim Donaghy happened to be refereeing. If the name does not sound familiar, let me give you the lowdown: The FBI investigated Donaghy for betting on basketball games, including some in which he had officiated. In the summer of 2007, he pleaded guilty to federal felony conspiracy charges alleging that he passed along inside information on NBA games.

That fateful Bulls-Knicks game was one of many games looked into by the FBI.

Kevin Garnett was eventually traded to the Boston Celtics in 2007 and that final piece of the puzzle enabled *them* to win the NBA championship. There is a silver lining in this black cloud: I don't bet on basketball anymore, let alone watch it.

Baseball

In 2006 I started watching a lot of Arizona Diamondbacks baseball games. They were on the local channels and the White Sox were only shown on WGN or ESPN occasionally. The Diamondbacks—or D-backs for short—played pretty well during the season with the exception of one long losing streak. In the middle of the summer they lost twenty-one out of twenty-three games, which basically put them out of contention for the division or the playoffs as a wild card team. Had they played .500 baseball during that streak, they would have made the playoffs.

The next year, 2007, I thought that the D-backs might be a good bet so I checked out the lines. I was amazed when they were quoted at 8 to 1 to win their division, 25 to 1 to win the National League Pennant, and 60 to 1 to win the World Series. I decided to invest $50 ($10 to win the division, $20 to win the pennant, and $20 to win the World Series). If they won the division, I'd show a small profit and have a free ride on the pennant and World Series. Winning it all would get me another $1,700.

Arizona played steady all year, avoiding any long losing streaks, and clinched the division on the second to last game of the year by beating the Colorado Rockies in Denver. Their final record was 90 wins and 72 losses—the best record in the National League, which assured them home-field advantage throughout the National League playoffs. The American League had secured home-field advantage in the World Series, by winning the All Star Game.

Arizona's manager, Bob Melvin, was brilliant all year, making all the right moves, until the last game of the regular season. In my opinion, he made a huge mistake resting most of the regulars during that game. Although this is common after clinching the division, this time it shouldn't have been done.

The Colorado Rockies were one of the hottest teams in baseball at that time, winning 11 out of 13 games. They needed a win in the last game against the D-backs, a San Diego Padres loss at Milwaukee, and then they had to go on the road and win a one-game playoff at San Diego to be the wildcard team. Almost like hitting the Trifecta.

Coach Melvin wasn't thinking that far ahead when he rested his players in the finale and they lost a close game 4 to 3 to the Rockies. Could they have won with their regular starters in the game? That's one thing we'll never know.

Milwaukee rallied to beat San Diego in their finale, and the hottest team in baseball was one win away from the playoffs. On Monday, Colorado beat San Diego to secure the playoff spot. Even though I collected my bet on Arizona winning the division, I was becoming increasingly leery about the Rockies.

Arizona was hosting the Chicago Cubs in the first round. The D-backs had no problem with the Cubs, so I was hoping that the Philadelphia Phillies could derail the runaway Rockies train. Unfortunately Colorado went through the Phillies like a knife through hot butter, sweeping them three straight.

As the saying goes: "Houston, we have a problem." The hottest team in baseball, winning 16 out of 18 games, was coming to Arizona and my confidence of cashing my two big bets was plummeting like the stocks in a bear market. I wonder if Bob Melvin was having second thoughts about that last game of the year. Maybe they should have postponed the celebration by one day and eliminated the Rockies from the playoffs on that fated Sunday.

Arizona had no chance to slow down the Colorado train, losing every game. I felt that one win against the Rockies would stop their momentum, and maybe turn the tide, but the one game the D-backs had a chance to win they instead gave away, by using their closer for sixty pitches (a no-no in baseball). By that time they were desperate for a win, so I couldn't blame them.

On the other hand the Boston Red Sox had no problem slowing down the hottest team in baseball (Rockies now having won 20 of 22). They beat Colorado four straight games to win the 2007 World Series.

In retrospect, had the Arizona Diamondbacks advanced to the 2007 World Series, they probably wouldn't have knocked off the

Red Sox, with a red hot line up that included future Hall of Famers Manny Ramirez and David Ortiz, as well as series MVP Mike Lowell. On the other hand, I would have had $500 in my pocket and 1,200 reasons (as in $1,200) to watch the World Series, which I avoided.

Betting sports is a tough gamble. The seasons are long and overlap. Having a bet on the season finale can be excruciating as well as exhilarating for months on end. My wife thinks I should try watching the games for the sport. What an interesting concept.

32

Could Today Be My Lucky Day?

After reading this book, you must be wondering if I have lost my mind. Why else would I continue to gamble? How many times must I lose "by a nose" before I truly realize and accept that winning at gambling may not be in my cards? Am I just a glutton for punishment? As Ricky Ricardo used to say, "Lucy, you have some explaining to do." So before you rush to judgment, let me explain.

Most gamblers just remember the wins and forget about their many losses along the way. I chose to emphasize the bad beats and almost wins because that is what the average gambler experiences. I have never been one to fool myself when it came to how much I was actually winning or losing—mostly losing! So why play if you can't win? The answer lies in what someone once told me at work a long time ago: "You never know if today is going to be your lucky day."

The Illinois Lottery had a similar slogan: "You can't win if you don't play." Although that statement is true, I would add the caveat "even though the lotto is a horrible bet."

Is today going to be my lucky day? That's what I ask myself all the time. The answer at the end of the day is usually a resounding "NO!" But then again, tomorrow's another day. There were some lucky days over the years, and like that birdie on the eighteenth hole after a bad round of golf, those days are what has kept me coming back for more. Here are a few lucky days that come to mind.

Meadowlake

After Arlington Park Racetrack burned down in 1985, the racing meet was held at Hawthorne Racetrack near Chicago. A lot of gamblers who frequented Arlington didn't want to venture into the city to play the ponies. Since there were no off-track betting parlors in existence at that time, people would sometimes send out bets with friends or tellers. Someone I knew asked me to bet $100 to win on a horse named Meadowlake who was running in the first race on that Friday. He forked over the cash and told me that the information was from a "good source" (where have I heard that before?). I told him that I would make the bet and he said "you better get some for yourself."

When I got to work I looked at the racing form and saw that his horse was a first-time starter and was listed at 20 to 1 odds in the program. First-time starters are normally bad bets, especially at long odds. Meadowlake opened up at 2 to 1 odds when the betting began. Did he really know something? I held off making the bet until closer to post time.

Meanwhile I was studying the form, looking for a horse or two in the second race, maybe at decent odds. Meadowlake was 3 to 1 at post time, so I decided to bet $90 to win and made two $5 doubles with horses that I liked in the second race.

I was technically on the hook for $10 to win on Meadowlake with the original wager being $100 and betting only $90. If the horse won, the most it would cost me was around $40 (because of the 3 to 1 odds) but then I would have two Daily Doubles going with my two picks in the second race. If the horse ran out—like most hot tips do—then no harm, no foul.

Meadowlake broke his maiden winning the first race easily and paid $8.60 to win. At this point, I owed $43 to make up the difference of $430 that the wager paid ($8.60 x 50) and the $387 I collected ($8.60 x 45). My saving grace was that I could recoup that and more if one of my Daily Doubles came in.

After the tote board posted the double payoffs on the horses in the second race, I had to look twice. The Daily Doubles were all good prices and my selections were paying $130 and $360. Those were the $2 payoffs; I had $5 doubles, which pay 2 ½ times. I stood to collect $325 and $900, depending on which horse won. What apparently happened was the money on Meadowlake was all in the win pool, not in the Daily Double pool. This happens a lot with "steamers" (hot horses who get bet down).

That day the racing gods were either smiling down on me, or they fell asleep at the wheel, because my $360 double came in netting me $857 ($900 minus $43, the difference owed on the original wager). The beauty was that I never took a dime out of my pocket. Somewhere Donald Trump was smiling.

After paying off the bettor, who was happy as a clam, he asked me if I got a little for myself. I could not help but smile and reply "I did okay."

The 1991 Chicago Bulls

The Chicago Bulls drafted Michael Jordan in the first round in 1984. From that year through 1986 the Bulls made the playoffs every year but were eliminated immediately, even though Jordan was spectacular. In 1987 the Bulls started to assemble a supporting cast around Jordan, drafting Horace Grant and trading for Scottie Pippen. In 1989 the final piece of the puzzle was put in place with the hiring of Phil Jackson as the new head coach.

The Bulls reached the conference semi-finals in 1989 and the finals in 1990, only to lose to the Detroit Pistons both times. But the Pistons were looking tired and I was convinced that the third time would be the charm for the Bulls. It was time to make a move.

Learning my lesson from the Chicago White Sox fiasco, I had to find someone going to Las Vegas. At the racetrack where I worked, you didn't have to wait more than a week or so to find someone who was making the trek west. I gave my friend Tom $100 and told him to get me the best price on the Bulls to win it all. I figured that if the Bulls were charmed and got by Detroit for the Eastern conference title, then beating the Western conference champs would be no problem.

When Tom came back and handed me the betting slip from the Imperial Palace, I was pleasantly surprised to be getting 9 to 1 odds on my wager. If the Bulls indeed won it all, I would collect a G-note or $1,000 ($900 plus my original wager of $100).

The Bulls reached the NBA finals in 1991 and easily won 11 of their 12 playoff games, with their only loss coming in the middle series to the Philadelphia Seventy-Sixers. When they swept their nemesis Detroit Pistons by winning four straight, I knew that the aging Los Angeles Lakers were doomed as well. Even with Magic Johnson and the Lakers winning the first game, I wasn't worried. The Bulls won the next four games, winning the NBA championship. They went on to win six out of the next eight titles. They were never close to the 9 to 1 odds I received in that future pool.

First Holdem Tournament Win

After 2000 I was not sure whether I would play in any more Holdem tournaments. That all changed in 2002 when Joy, a friend from the racetrack, told me about a group of her friends that held seven-card stud tournaments and wanted to know if I was interested in playing. I told her that I was not much of a stud player, but I would give it a shot.

The game was being held at a house not too far from where I lived. When I showed up everybody was friendly, but I didn't last very long and got knocked out in a couple of hours. Before leaving, I talked to a few of the guys about playing Holdem next time and they seemed interested.

In September Joy told me that they were having their first Holdem tournament and I was invited. It didn't hurt that I was easy meat at the last game. I think that they smelled fresh fish again. Over thirty guys showed up for the roasting, and at $150 a pop (entry fee) the winner's cut was $2,200. They paid the top five; so I didn't have to win it all to make some money, just hit the board.

I got there early for the game and parked my car right by the front door, so all could see my license plate as they entered. One by one as they filed in they all asked the same question: "Who's driving the Nissan with the 'HOLDEM 6' license plate?" Each time I peered through the top of my sunglasses, beneath my Binions World Series of Poker hat, and replied, "That would be me."

One thing I learned from playing poker in Las Vegas tournaments was that table presence means a lot. If people fear you or think that you are a better player, this will give you a tremendous advantage. You can bluff more, steal some pots, and you get to see more cards after the flop, as players are afraid to raise you. That night I had the table presence of Stu Unger, the only player to win the big World Series of Poker tournament three times.

Winning my first Holdem tournament that evening was a thrill. They even had my name put on the plaque on the wall as the first Holdem winner, right next to the seven-card stud champions. That Holdem license plate had been on my car for twelve years and it finally paid off.

2005 World Series Champion Chicago White Sox

As Yogi Berra once said, "It's déjà vu all over again." The Chicago White Sox went 99 and 63 in 1983 after an improving season the previous year (87 and 75). In 2004 the Sox hired Ozzie Guillen to manage the team and went on to win 83 games. The Sox were on the rise. Ozzie, as everyone on the South Side referred to him, had a fiery personality. He made his predecessors look like undertakers. "The Blizzard of Oz" was another moniker he acquired pretty quickly.

The White Sox had good spring training in 2005 and jumped out to a good start for the season. They went 4 and 2 in their first six games against Cleveland and Minnesota, their biggest division rivalries. I was talking baseball with Tony one day and he told me he could get me a bet down if I was interested in betting the Sox. I had dealt with Tony before getting bets down and he was good as gold, so I wasn't worried about getting paid or needing a receipt.

After checking out the future bets, it was obvious the Sox were still not getting any respect with odds of 22 to 1 to win the pennant and 45 to 1 to win the World Series. I could not believe that the line had not moved after their good start, so I invested $40. The days of betting a G-note were gone but not forgotten. I gave Tony the $40 and told him to bet $20 on the pennant and $20 on the World Series. I would throw away 40 hogs for a chance at collecting $1,380.

The White Sox ended up with the best record in April. By the All Star break in July they had 57 wins and only 29 losses, and held a commanding nine-game lead for first place in their division. I had yet to attend a game, as I didn't want to jinx them. With a 15-game lead on August 1, it seemed safe enough for me to catch a few games at U.S. Cellular Field. I went to my first game on August 15 and their first-place lead had slipped to 11 games. By my second appearance at the ballpark on August 21, their first-place lead was 8 ½ games and plummeting.

By September 22, the White Sox clung to a lead of 1 ½ games and *Chicago Sun-Times* sports columnist Jay Mariotti, a notorious Sox loather, was writing the team's obituary. I vowed not to go near the ballpark, even if it meant missing a playoff game. My prayers were answered as the White Sox won 8 of their last 10 games to finish the season with a 99 and 63 record—the same record as 1983. Déjà vu?

The White Sox had led their division every step of the way from the first game to the last, a rare feat in baseball. That momentum carried through the playoffs and the World Series as their 11 and 1 post-season record tied the New York Yankees as the best ever.

I kept my promise and did not go to one playoff or World Series game. Sam, my brother Jerry, and I watched some of the games together at Sam's house, but none of us wanted to be the jinx. I had no problem collecting $1,380 from Tony (good as gold), and retired and moved the next week. That's leaving town on a high note.

Who is J.B. Holmes . . .

. . . and what does he have to do with me? As my Uncle Dick would say, "Give me the story." So here it is. J.B. Holmes is a golfer who turned pro in late 2005, playing in one tournament that year and winning no money. In 2006 he started out the season finishing tenth in the Sony open, withdrew from the Bob Hope Desert Classic the next week, and then tied for twenty-eighth in the Buick Invitational the following week.

The first week in February he was playing in the FBR Open in Phoenix, Arizona. I was not watching the tournament that week, and even if I were watching it, I wouldn't have known J.B. Holmes from Adam.

Almost all golf tournaments start on Thursday and run four days through Sunday. The cut is made after day two with about half the field advancing. The one unique thing about golf tournaments is that if you don't make the cut, you don't get paid. Everyone who makes the cut gets a check, with the lion's share going to the top ten golfers.

On Friday afternoon, Tony called and asked me if I was watching the FBR Open. When I told him I was not, he told me to go to the PGA website and check out a new feature called the tour cam. You could follow your favorite player, even if they were not showing him on TV. It was a free promotion to try to get people interested in the feature. After the tournament it would only be available for a monthly fee.

The one golfer Tony was following on the tour cam was J.B. Holmes, who had shot a 68 (3 under par) on the first day. He was 7 under par on Friday's round and leading the tournament. Tony told me that J.B. Holmes's tee shots averaged 315 yards and that he had a great iron game, too. Since Tony caddied for a pro in his younger days, he knew a thing or two about the game of golf.

The other thing that Tony knew was how to spot an overlay. Similar to E.F. Hutton, when he talked, you listened. At the time the golf shares on J.B. Holmes were selling for $5 each, which, in Tony's opinion, was a real overlay. As the shares were redeemable for $100, you were basically getting 20 to 1 odds on the leader halfway through the tournament. You would like to have your horse leading the race at those odds every time! Even if Holmes was a rookie, they all have to break their maiden sooner or later. The fact that Holmes blasted the ball off the tees gave him a distinct advantage on a desert courses without a lot of trees.

After day two, J.B. Holmes was still the leader at 10 under par and I decided to buy ten shares. When I went to purchase them they had gone up to $7 a share so I invested $70 on the advice of my "E. F. Hutton." I wondered if it was Tony who moved the shares up.

On Saturday, after running a few errands, I came home and checked the leader board. My man had shot a 65 and remained in the lead with 16 under par. Suddenly, someone whom I had never even heard of days earlier, was now "my man." I checked my shares and they were up to $40 each. I sold two, recouping my original investment plus $10, and now I was on a free ride for $800.

That Sunday I just sat back and enjoyed the ride as J.B. Holmes, a virtual unknown, shot a 66 to put him 21 under par for the tournament win. To this day, Holmes has never shot another 21 under par, and it took him two years to win his second PGA tournament, the same FBR Open (go figure).

In retrospect, that Sunday was one of my lucky days.

Epilogue

Do as I Say, *Not* as I Do

After forty-five years of gambling, including thirty years of working at racetracks, there is not much that has escaped me when it comes to betting. I may have seen it all and, possibly, done most of it.

My first $88 Quinella hooked me on horseracing, and the $20 bill from my grandmother's Catholic Missal led to my first big poker win. I've been betting horses and playing poker ever since. Along my journey I also dabbled in wagering on baseball, football (pro and college), basketball (pro and college), golf, and dog racing. I drew the line on hockey and boxing, which really didn't interest me.

Betting on dog racing was something I did rarely and for entertainment purposes only. Watching dogs chase a fake bone around a track and running over each other was good for a few laughs. My Uncle Will in Florida had what he dubbed the "Chinese System." He'd look for a dog in the first race whose name started with an "A" and then bet that puppy. If there wasn't one, he'd move on to "B" and so on and so forth. Will followed this format all the way through the alphabet and the races. After making all the bets he would go play poker, not even bothering to watch. He did better than the rest of us with his "system."

However, if the dogs happened to float your boat, you'd probably do just as well betting your birth date or any lucky number and hoping for the best. I've never met or heard of anyone who has made a living betting on dogs. Charlie the Pool Closer was the only bettor I've ever known who even attempted to beat the game.

After more than four decades of betting thoroughbred horses, I've come full circle. I started out betting races on my day off—Saturday—with the rest of the tourists. After honing my skills, I tried swimming with the sharks (the pros) and bet on weekdays. Ironically, I now believe that weekends, holidays, and special days (Derby, Breeders' Cup) are the way to go to find an overlay among the family favorites. Overlays are basically horses that go off at higher odds than their form would indicate. This happens when everybody bets "Uncle Joe's Namesake" instead of a horse with real potential.

One bet that I've had some success with and mentioned before is betting on "futures." This is popular in Las Vegas for sports like football, baseball, and basketball. You can also pick teams to win pennants, divisions, or conferences and titles. The best part of betting futures is you don't have to bet the individual games and still have action for the whole season, or until your team is eliminated. With wildcards in baseball and football, you could get down to the last week of the season and still have a rooting interest.

Gambling, like most anything, should be done in moderation. The problem is that, like anything addictive, it's often hard to practice restraint. When winning, there's a high that keeps the gambler playing; losing pushes gamblers to keep playing to reclaim that high and get their money back. Gambling can also become obsessive and alter some gamblers' moods. The highs experienced when winning are never as low as the lows are when losing.

They say that God worked six days and rested on the seventh. For some gamblers, it would be better to bet one day and rest the other six. I suggest picking your vice of choice and one day a week gamble whatever you can afford to lose. A total loss is considered entertainment and a win is getting paid to be entertained.

If college football is your bag, bet it on Saturday and forget the pro games on Sunday. If you're more apt to bet the pros, then stick to Sunday and forget about Monday Night Football.

Always keep bets consistent. Set an amount and stick to it regardless of wins or losses. Murphy's Law tends to deliver losses with big bets and wins with the small bets. Stay consistent and Murphy can kiss your ass. Streak gamblers should capitalize on the rushes. Bet only a specific percentage of your bankroll. A win would increase the next bet and a loss would decrease it. This way you would preserve your bankroll longer when losing and get more out of the winning streak. Discipline is the key here.

What I do know is that gambling can be very destructive and costly. I have four golden rules I recommend:

1) Gambling can be a *part of* your life, but it should *not be* your life.
2) Never gamble what you can't afford to lose.
3) Never let it interfere with any of your relationships.
4) When it stops being fun it's time to quit.

About 5 percent of gamblers have the right to call themselves professionals and make a living at it. The other 95 percent of us are just building the new casinos or buying the bookmakers those new Cadillacs.

At the beginning of this book I didn't realize how much fun I would have walking down memory lane. Recalling all the "good old days" has been a blast. What is even more surprising is that I've discovered I don't have to bet on *my* team to enjoy watching the game, imagine that.

In the end, my father Vince said it best:

> We are not here for a long time,
> We are here for a good time.

Amen.

RACE 9   May 20, 1990   RACE 9   May 20, 1990

MIRROR IMAGE

DEAD HEAT

WIN
EYE IN THE SKY

Photo of a rare
three horse dead heat